OpenGL Deep Dive: Expert Techniques and Performance Optimization

OpenGL

Kameron Hussain and Frahaan Hussain

Published by Sonar Publishing, 2023.

While every precaution has been taken in the preparation of this book, the publisher assumes no responsibility for errors or omissions, or for damages resulting from the use of the information contained herein.

OPENGL DEEP DIVE: EXPERT TECHNIQUES AND PERFORMANCE OPTIMIZATION

First edition. October 16, 2023.

ISBN: 979-8215411308

Written by Kameron Hussain and Frahaan Hussain.

Table of Contents

8. Audio Shaders and Processing:

9. Accessibility Considerations:

10. Future Potential:

Section 10.2: Real-time Reverberation Techniques

1. Importance of Reverberation:

2. Convolution Reverb:

3. Real-time Convolution:

4. Parameterization and Control:

5. Spatialization and Reverberation:

6. Interactive Environments:

7. Hardware Acceleration:

8. Future Trends:

9. Integration Challenges:

10. Audio Rendering Engines:

Section 10.3: Advanced Audio Simulation

1. Physical Modeling:

2. Wave-Based Simulation:

3. Dynamic Environmental Audio:

4. Sound Propagation:

5. Binaural Audio:

6. Real-time DSP Effects:

7. HRTF (Head-Related Transfer Function):

8. Audio Occlusion and Diffraction:

9. Dynamic Mixing and Spatialization:

10. Performance Considerations:

11. Middleware and Audio Engines:

12. User Experience Enhancement:

Section 10.4: Sound Propagation in Complex Environments

1. Geometric Acoustics:

2. Ray Tracing:

3. Materials and Absorption:

4. Reverberation:

5. Convolution and Impulse Responses:

6. Dynamic Environments:

7. Computational Complexity:

8. Middleware and Audio Engines:

9. Real-time Ray Tracing:

10. Immersive Audio Experiences:

Section 10.5: Audio Shaders and Processing

1. Audio Shaders Overview:

2. Dynamic Sound Generation:

3. Real-time Filters and Effects:

4. Spatial Audio:

5. Doppler Effect and Velocity:

6. Environmental Audio:

7. Dynamic Mixing and Balancing:

8. Audio Synthesis:

9. Performance Optimization:

10. Integration with Game Engines:

11. Cross-platform Compatibility:

12. Future Trends:

Chapter 11: Procedural Generation Techniques

Section 11.1: Procedural Modelling and Texturing

Procedural Modeling

Procedural Texturing

Section 11.2: Infinite Worlds and Fractal Geometry

Understanding Fractal Geometry

Generating Infinite Worlds

Section 11.3: Advanced Terrain Generation

Heightmap-Based Terrain Generation

Chapter 16: Toolchain and Workflow Mastery

Section 16.1: Advanced Debugging Techniques

1. Debugging Graphics Shaders

2. Real-time Debugging

3. Memory Debugging

4. Crash Analysis

5. Collaborative Debugging

6. Advanced Debugging Tips

7. Post-mortem Analysis

8. Continuous Integration for Debugging

9. Conclusion

Section 16.2: Continuous Integration for Graphics Projects

1. Benefits of CI for Graphics Projects

2. Setting Up a CI Pipeline

3. Rendering Tests

4. Performance Benchmarks

5. Deployment

6. Conclusion

Section 16.3: Shader and Asset Pipelining

Section 19.4: Open Source and Community Contributions

1. Collaborative Development

2. Accessibility

3. Transparency and Trust

4. Community Support

5. Learning Opportunities

6. Customization and Extensibility

7. Community Diversity

8. Leveraging Existing Work

9. Contributing Back

10. Ethical Considerations

Section 19.5: Ensuring Future Tech is Inclusive

1. Accessibility Matters

2. Legal and Ethical Obligations

3. Universal Design Principles

4. Testing with Diverse User Groups

5. Accessible User Interfaces

6. Captioning and Transcripts

7. Keyboard Navigation

8. Performance Considerations

Chapter 1: Optimization Fundamentals

Section 1.1: Profiling Your OpenGL Application

Profiling your OpenGL application is a crucial step in optimizing its performance. Profiling helps you identify bottlenecks and areas where improvements can be made. In this section, we will explore various profiling techniques and tools that can assist you in the optimization process.

Profiling can be broadly categorized into two types: CPU profiling and GPU profiling. CPU profiling involves analyzing the performance of your application's CPU-bound tasks, while GPU profiling focuses on the GPU's performance and how it interacts with your application. Let's dive into these two aspects in more detail.

CPU Profiling

When it comes to CPU profiling, you can use various tools to gather data on your application's execution. One popular tool is **perf**, a command-line profiler for Linux systems. Here's a simple example of how to use perf to profile your OpenGL application:

```
$ perf record -e cycles:u -g ./your_opengl_app
```

In this command, we use **perf record** to record performance data. The **-e** flag specifies the event we want to count, in this case, CPU cycles. The **-g** flag records call graphs, which can be invaluable for pinpointing bottlenecks in your code. Replace **./your_opengl_app** with the actual executable of your OpenGL application.

Once the profiling is complete, you can use **perf report** to analyze the collected data:

$ perf report

This generates a report that shows where your application spent most of its CPU cycles, helping you identify performance bottlenecks.

GPU Profiling

GPU profiling is essential for optimizing OpenGL applications, as the GPU plays a significant role in rendering graphics. Tools like NVIDIA's **Nsight Graphics** and AMD's **Radeon GPU Profiler** can provide valuable insights into your application's GPU performance.

These tools allow you to capture GPU traces, view the timeline of GPU events, and analyze shader performance. You can identify issues such as shader compilation times, inefficient GPU resource usage, and synchronization problems.

Summary

Profiling your OpenGL application is the first step towards optimization. Whether you focus on CPU or GPU profiling, using the right tools and techniques will help you identify and address performance bottlenecks. In the subsequent sections of this chapter, we will delve deeper into specific optimization strategies and techniques to improve your OpenGL application's performance.

Section 1.2: Bottleneck Analysis

Bottleneck analysis is a critical aspect of optimizing OpenGL applications. Identifying and addressing bottlenecks can significantly improve the overall performance of your graphics software. In this section, we'll explore how to conduct bottleneck analysis and discuss common bottlenecks you may encounter.

Conducting Bottleneck Analysis

Bottleneck analysis involves the following steps:

1. **Profiling:** Before you can identify bottlenecks, you need to profile your application, as discussed in the previous section. Profiling provides data on CPU and GPU usage, rendering times, and other performance metrics.
2. **Data Analysis:** Once you have profiling data, it's time to analyze it. Look for areas where your application spends a significant amount of time or resources. Common metrics to consider include frame rendering times, shader compilation times, and CPU/GPU utilization.
3. **Benchmarking:** Benchmarking involves running your application under various conditions to assess its performance. You can benchmark different scenes, settings, or hardware configurations to pinpoint performance variations and bottlenecks.
4. **Identifying Bottlenecks:** Based on your analysis and benchmarking results, identify bottlenecks. These are specific areas or operations in your code that cause performance degradation. Common bottlenecks include inefficient shaders, excessive CPU-GPU synchronization, and memory allocation issues.
5. **Optimization:** Once you've identified bottlenecks, work on optimizing them. This may involve rewriting shaders, reducing CPU-GPU synchronization points, optimizing data structures, or using more efficient algorithms.

Common Bottlenecks in OpenGL Applications

Let's explore some common bottlenecks you may encounter in OpenGL applications:

1. Shader Performance:

Shaders are a fundamental part of graphics rendering, and poorly optimized shaders can be a significant bottleneck. Look for inefficient shader code, redundant calculations, and unused variables. Consider using shader profiling tools to identify performance bottlenecks within your shaders.

2. CPU-GPU Synchronization:

Excessive synchronization between the CPU and GPU can lead to performance issues. Minimize the use of functions like glFinish and glFlush as they introduce synchronization points. Consider using asynchronous rendering techniques to overlap CPU and GPU work.

3. Texture Management:

Inefficient texture management can impact performance. Avoid frequent texture uploads to the GPU and minimize texture changes during rendering. Consider using texture atlases or texture arrays to reduce the number of texture bindings.

4. Memory Management:

Inefficient memory allocation and deallocation can slow down your application. Profile memory usage and look for memory leaks or excessive allocations. Consider using memory pools or reuse strategies to optimize memory usage.

5. State Changes:

Frequent OpenGL state changes can degrade performance. Minimize the number of state changes by grouping similar rendering operations together. Use techniques like instancing to reduce state changes when rendering multiple instances of the same object.

Conclusion

Bottleneck analysis is a crucial step in optimizing OpenGL applications. By profiling, analyzing data, benchmarking, identifying bottlenecks, and implementing optimizations, you can enhance the performance and efficiency of your graphics software. In the subsequent sections of this chapter, we'll explore more advanced optimization techniques to tackle specific bottlenecks.

Section 1.3: GPU and CPU Synchronization

Synchronization between the CPU and GPU is a critical aspect of optimizing OpenGL applications. Efficient synchronization ensures that both the CPU and GPU work together seamlessly to maximize performance. In this section, we will delve into the nuances of GPU and CPU synchronization and explore strategies for optimizing it.

Understanding CPU-GPU Interaction

Modern graphics applications involve complex interactions between the CPU and GPU. The CPU is responsible for sending rendering commands to the GPU, while the GPU processes these commands and produces the final image. Synchronization points occur when the CPU and GPU need to coordinate their actions.

Common synchronization points include:

1. **glFinish:** This OpenGL function ensures that all previously issued commands have completed execution on the GPU before allowing the CPU to proceed. While it guarantees synchronization, it can introduce significant stalls and negatively impact performance.
2. **glFlush:** Unlike glFinish, glFlush ensures that previously issued commands are sent to the GPU but does not wait for their completion. It can help reduce stalls but does not provide strong synchronization.

Strategies for Optimizing CPU-GPU Synchronization

To optimize CPU-GPU synchronization, consider the following strategies:

1. Asynchronous Rendering:

One of the most effective strategies is to minimize the use of glFinish and glFlush by adopting asynchronous rendering techniques. Instead of waiting for the GPU to finish processing, the CPU can continue issuing commands for subsequent frames or tasks. This approach can significantly improve overall throughput.

// Enabling asynchronous rendering

glFlush(); *// Can be used to submit commands to the GPU*

2. Buffering and Pipelining:

Implement buffering and pipelining mechanisms to overlap CPU and GPU work. For example, you can use double or triple buffering to have multiple frames in flight simultaneously. This allows the CPU to work on generating the next frame while the GPU is rendering the current one.

// Using double buffering

glSwapBuffers(); *// Swap the front and back buffers*

3. Multi-threading:

If your application allows for it, consider using multi-threading to offload CPU tasks to separate threads. This can help keep the CPU busy with other tasks while the GPU is rendering. However, be cautious with multi-threading, as improper synchronization between threads can introduce new synchronization bottlenecks.

// Example of multi-threading in C++

std::thread renderingThread(RenderFrame);

renderingThread.join(); *// Wait for the rendering thread to finish*

4. Minimize State Changes:

Frequent OpenGL state changes can lead to synchronization points. Minimize the number of state changes by grouping similar rendering operations together. Use techniques like batching to reduce the need for state changes between draw calls.

// Example of minimizing state changes

```
glBindTexture(GL_TEXTURE_2D, texture1);

glDrawElements(GL_TRIANGLES, ...);

glBindTexture(GL_TEXTURE_2D, texture2);

glDrawElements(GL_TRIANGLES, ...);
```

Conclusion

Efficient CPU-GPU synchronization is crucial for achieving high performance in OpenGL applications. By adopting asynchronous rendering, buffering, multi-threading, and minimizing state changes, you can optimize synchronization and improve the overall responsiveness and frame rates of your graphics software. In the subsequent sections, we will explore more advanced optimization techniques to further enhance your OpenGL applications.

Section 1.4: Batch Rendering Techniques

Batch rendering is a fundamental optimization technique in OpenGL that can significantly improve rendering performance by reducing CPU-GPU synchronization overhead. In this section, we will explore the concept of batch rendering and various strategies to implement it effectively in your OpenGL applications.

Understanding Batch Rendering

Batch rendering involves grouping multiple rendering operations together into a single draw call. Instead of issuing individual draw calls for each object or primitive, you collect similar objects or geometry into batches and render them in a single pass. This minimizes the overhead associated with CPU-GPU synchronization, state changes, and draw calls.

Benefits of Batch Rendering

Batch rendering offers several key benefits:

1. **Reduced CPU Overhead:** By minimizing the number of draw calls, you reduce the CPU's workload, allowing it to focus on other tasks such as physics calculations or AI processing.
2. **Minimized State Changes:** Batch rendering allows you to maintain a consistent rendering state within a single draw call, reducing the need for costly state changes between draw calls.
3. **Improved GPU Efficiency:** The GPU can process batches more efficiently because it can optimize its internal pipeline for rendering similar objects.

Strategies for Implementing Batch Rendering

To implement batch rendering effectively, consider the following strategies:

1. Object Sorting:

Before rendering, sort the objects or geometry by their rendering properties, such as material, shader, or texture. Objects with similar properties should be grouped together in batches. This ensures that state changes are minimized within each batch.

// Example of sorting objects by material

```
std::sort(objects.begin(), objects.end(), CompareByMaterial);
```

2. Vertex Buffer Objects (VBOs):

Use Vertex Buffer Objects to store vertex data on the GPU. VBOs allow you to upload and manage geometry data efficiently. When rendering batches, you can bind the appropriate VBOs for each batch, reducing data transfer overhead between the CPU and GPU.

```
// Example of using VBOs

glGenBuffers(1, &vbo);

glBindBuffer(GL_ARRAY_BUFFER, vbo);

glBufferData(GL_ARRAY_BUFFER, sizeof(vertices), vertices, GL_STATIC_DRAW);
```

3. Uniform Buffer Objects (UBOs):

For shared rendering properties such as transformation matrices or material parameters, consider using Uniform Buffer Objects. UBOs allow you to update uniform data once and share it among multiple objects within a batch.

```
// Example of using UBOs

glGenBuffers(1, &ubo);

glBindBuffer(GL_UNIFORM_BUFFER, ubo);

glBufferData(GL_UNIFORM_BUFFER, sizeof(UniformData), &data, GL_DYNAMIC_DRAW);
```

4. Instanced Rendering:

Instanced rendering is a technique that allows you to render multiple instances of the same object with a single draw call. It is especially useful for rendering large numbers of identical objects, such as particles or instances in a scene.

```
// Example of instanced rendering

glDrawElementsInstanced(GL_TRIANGLES, numIndices, GL_UNSIGNED_INT, 0, numInstances);
```

Conclusion

Batch rendering is a powerful optimization technique in OpenGL that can significantly improve rendering performance by reducing CPU-GPU synchronization overhead. By sorting objects, using VBOs, UBOs, and instanced rendering, you can implement batch rendering effectively and enhance the efficiency of your OpenGL applications. In the following sections, we will explore more advanced optimization techniques to further optimize your graphics software.

Section 1.5: Reducing State Changes

Reducing state changes is a critical aspect of optimizing OpenGL applications. Excessive state changes can introduce synchronization overhead and degrade performance. In this section, we will explore strategies for minimizing state changes and improving the efficiency of your OpenGL rendering pipeline.

Understanding OpenGL State

OpenGL maintains a vast amount of rendering state, including settings for rendering modes, blending, depth testing, and texture bindings. Each time you change one of these states, OpenGL may need to perform internal work to accommodate the change. These state changes can become bottlenecks, especially if they occur frequently during rendering.

Strategies for Minimizing State Changes

To reduce state changes effectively, consider the following strategies:

1. State Sorting:

Before rendering objects, sort them based on their rendering properties, such as shaders, materials, and textures. Group objects with the same rendering state together to minimize state changes within rendering batches.

```
// Example of sorting objects by shader

std::sort(objects.begin(), objects.end(), CompareByShader);
```

2. Texture Atlases and Texture Arrays:

Instead of binding individual textures for each object, consider using texture atlases or texture arrays. These techniques allow you to combine multiple textures into a single texture unit, reducing the number of texture bindings.

```
// Example of using a texture atlas

glBindTexture(GL_TEXTURE_2D, textureAtlas);
```

3. Shader Programs:

Minimize shader program changes by grouping objects that use the same shader program together. Switching shader programs involves a costly state change, so optimizing this can lead to significant performance gains.

// Example of using a shader program

glUseProgram(shaderProgram);

4. Uniform Buffer Objects (UBOs):

Use Uniform Buffer Objects to store shared rendering properties such as transformation matrices or lighting information. UBOs allow you to update uniform data once and share it among multiple objects within a batch.

// Example of using UBOs

glGenBuffers(1, &ubo);

glBindBuffer(GL_UNIFORM_BUFFER, ubo);

glBufferData(GL_UNIFORM_BUFFER,   **sizeof**(UniformData), &data, GL_DYNAMIC_DRAW);

5. Render-to-Texture Techniques:

When using multiple render passes or post-processing effects, minimize framebuffer switches. Implement render-to-texture techniques that allow you to reuse framebuffers and render targets, reducing state changes associated with framebuffer switches.

// Example of rendering to a texture

```
glBindFramebuffer(GL_FRAMEBUFFER, framebuffer);
```

State Change Impact Analysis

Profiling and analyzing the impact of state changes on your application's performance are crucial steps. Profiling tools can help identify which state changes have the most significant impact on rendering performance, allowing you to prioritize optimization efforts.

Conclusion

Reducing state changes is a key optimization technique in OpenGL. By sorting objects, using texture atlases, minimizing shader program changes, utilizing UBOs, and implementing efficient framebuffer management, you can minimize state changes and improve the efficiency of your OpenGL rendering pipeline. In the subsequent sections, we will explore more advanced optimization techniques to further enhance your graphics software.

Chapter 2: Advanced GPU Techniques

Section 2.1: Compute Shaders in Depth

Compute shaders are a powerful feature in modern GPUs that allow for highly parallelized data processing tasks beyond traditional rendering. In this section, we will delve into compute shaders, their capabilities, and how to use them effectively in your OpenGL applications.

Understanding Compute Shaders

Compute shaders are a type of shader program that run on the GPU but are not limited to graphics tasks. They are designed for general-purpose computing and can perform a wide range of calculations, such as physics simulations, data processing, and procedural content generation. Compute shaders are particularly well-suited for tasks that can be parallelized.

Compute Shader Basics

Here's a basic overview of compute shaders in OpenGL:

- **Shader Type:** Compute shaders are a distinct shader type, separate from vertex and fragment shaders. They are written in GLSL (OpenGL Shading Language), just like other shader types.

- **Data Dispatch:** Compute shaders are dispatched by the CPU using a function called glDispatchCompute(). This function specifies the number of workgroups and threads to execute.

// Dispatch a compute shader with 64 workgroups of 256 threads each

glDispatchCompute(64, 1, 1);

- **Thread Hierarchy:** Compute shaders work in a hierarchical thread model, with workgroups containing multiple threads. Threads within a workgroup can synchronize and share data using shared memory.

- **Data Storage:** Compute shaders can read and write data to various storage locations, including buffer objects, texture images, and image load/store operations.

- **Memory Barriers:** Proper memory synchronization is essential in compute shaders. Memory barriers are used to ensure memory consistency between threads.

Use Cases for Compute Shaders

Compute shaders have a wide range of use cases, including:

1. **Physics Simulations:** Compute shaders can simulate complex physical phenomena like fluid dynamics, particle systems, and cloth simulations.
2. **Procedural Content Generation:** Generate procedural textures, terrain, or geometry using compute shaders. They excel at creating detailed and randomized content.
3. **Data Processing:** Compute shaders are ideal for data processing tasks, such as image and signal processing, data compression, and cryptography.
4. **Parallel Algorithms:** Implement parallel algorithms for tasks like sorting, searching, and machine learning computations.

5. **Post-processing Effects:** Compute shaders can be used for post-processing effects like bloom, depth of field, and ambient occlusion.

Writing Compute Shaders

Writing a compute shader involves defining the shader's inputs, outputs, and operations. Compute shaders have a global invocation ID that allows each thread to know its position within the workgroup, which is useful for processing data in parallel.

Here's a simplified example of a compute shader that adds two arrays element-wise:

```
layout(std430, binding = 0) buffer InputBufferA {

float data[];

};

layout(std430, binding = 1) buffer InputBufferB {

float data[];

};

layout(std430, binding = 2) buffer OutputBuffer {

float result[];

};

void main() {

uint index = gl_GlobalInvocationID.x;

result[index] = data[index] + data[index];
```

}

Conclusion

Compute shaders offer a versatile and powerful way to leverage the GPU for general-purpose computations. Understanding their basics, thread model, and memory synchronization is crucial for harnessing their potential. In the following sections, we will explore more advanced GPU techniques, including GPGPU programming and direct memory access.

Section 2.2: GPGPU (General Purpose GPU) Programming

GPGPU programming is a specialized field that harnesses the computational power of GPUs for general-purpose tasks. It allows you to offload non-graphics computations to the GPU, which can significantly accelerate certain types of workloads. In this section, we will explore GPGPU programming, its benefits, and how to get started with it using OpenGL.

Benefits of GPGPU Programming

GPGPU programming offers several advantages:

1. **Parallelism:** GPUs are highly parallel processors with thousands of cores, making them ideal for tasks that can be parallelized. GPGPU programming allows you to take advantage of this parallelism.
2. **Performance:** GPUs can perform certain computations much faster than CPUs, especially for tasks like matrix operations, simulations, and machine learning.
3. **Energy Efficiency:** GPUs are designed to be energy-efficient, making them a cost-effective solution for

computationally intensive tasks.

4. **Graphics Integration:** GPGPU programming can be seamlessly integrated into existing OpenGL applications, allowing you to leverage both graphics and general-purpose computation capabilities.

GPGPU with OpenGL

OpenGL provides a standardized and widely supported framework for GPGPU programming through compute shaders, as discussed in the previous section. Here's a high-level overview of how to perform GPGPU programming with OpenGL:

1. **Create Compute Shaders:** Write compute shader programs that define the computation you want to perform on the GPU. These shaders are separate from the rendering pipeline and can be loaded and compiled at runtime.

2. **Set Up Buffers:** Create buffer objects (e.g., SSBOs - Shader Storage Buffer Objects) to store input and output data for your compute shaders. These buffers can be read from and written to by the shaders.

3. **Dispatch Compute:** Use glDispatchCompute() to dispatch the compute shaders, specifying the number of workgroups and threads. Each thread executes the shader code in parallel.

4. **Memory Barriers:** Implement memory barriers in your shaders to ensure proper synchronization when reading and writing data from buffers.

5. **Retrieve Results:** After dispatching the compute shaders, you can read the results from the output buffer objects back to the CPU for further processing or visualization.

Example Use Cases

GPGPU programming is applicable to various use cases, including:

- **Scientific Simulations:** Simulating physical phenomena like fluid dynamics, particle interactions, and simulations in scientific research.

- **Image and Video Processing:** Accelerating image and video processing tasks, such as image filtering, convolution, and video encoding/decoding.

- **Machine Learning:** Training and inference for machine learning models using GPU-accelerated libraries like TensorFlow and CUDA.

- **Numerical Computing:** Performing numerical computations like matrix operations, Fourier transforms, and solving differential equations.

Getting Started

To get started with GPGPU programming in OpenGL:

1. Set up your OpenGL context and load your compute shaders.
2. Create and configure buffer objects (SSBOs) to hold input and output data.
3. Dispatch your compute shaders using glDispatchCompute() with appropriate workgroup sizes.
4. Implement proper memory barriers to ensure data consistency.
5. Retrieve and process the results as needed.

Conclusion

GPGPU programming is a valuable tool for offloading computationally intensive tasks to the GPU, taking advantage of its parallel processing capabilities. With OpenGL's support for compute shaders and buffer objects, you can seamlessly integrate GPGPU programming into your graphics applications, opening up new possibilities for acceleration and optimization. In the following sections, we will explore more advanced GPU techniques and direct memory access (DMA).

Section 2.3: Direct Memory Access and Persistence

Direct Memory Access (DMA) and memory persistence are advanced GPU techniques that can significantly improve data transfer and memory management in OpenGL applications. In this section, we will explore these techniques and their benefits.

Understanding Direct Memory Access (DMA)

DMA is a mechanism that allows the GPU to directly access and transfer data between the CPU and GPU memory without involving the CPU in the data transfer process. Traditionally, when data needed to be transferred from CPU to GPU or vice versa, the CPU was responsible for initiating and managing the transfer. DMA bypasses this involvement, making data transfers more efficient.

Benefits of DMA

DMA offers several advantages for OpenGL applications:

1. **Reduced CPU Overhead:** By offloading data transfer tasks to the GPU, DMA reduces the CPU's involvement

in data transfers. This frees up the CPU to perform other tasks, improving overall application performance.

2. **Faster Data Transfers:** DMA can transfer data between CPU and GPU memory at higher speeds than traditional CPU-driven transfers. This is particularly beneficial for large datasets.

3. **Parallelism:** DMA allows data transfers to occur in parallel with other GPU tasks, improving overall system throughput.

Memory Persistence

Memory persistence is a related concept that allows data to remain resident in GPU memory across multiple frames. In traditional OpenGL, data sent to the GPU would often be evicted from GPU memory after rendering, requiring re-uploading for subsequent frames. Memory persistence ensures that data remains in GPU memory as long as it is needed, reducing the need for frequent data transfers.

Using DMA and Memory Persistence

To leverage DMA and memory persistence in OpenGL, you can use techniques and features such as:

1. **Persistent Buffer Mapping:** OpenGL provides functions like glMapBufferRange() with the GL_MAP_PERSISTENT_BIT flag, which allows you to map a buffer into CPU address space and ensure its persistence in GPU memory.

// Example of persistent buffer mapping

GLuint buffer;

```
glGenBuffers(1, &buffer);

glBindBuffer(GL_ARRAY_BUFFER, buffer);

glBufferStorage(GL_ARRAY_BUFFER, size, data,
GL_MAP_WRITE_BIT                            |
GL_MAP_PERSISTENT_BIT);

void*                 mappedData                 =
glMapBufferRange(GL_ARRAY_BUFFER,    0,    size,
GL_MAP_WRITE_BIT                            |
GL_MAP_PERSISTENT_BIT);
```

1. **Texture Storage:** Texture objects can also benefit from memory persistence. Use functions like glTexStorage2D() to allocate texture memory with the GL_MAP_PERSISTENT_BIT flag.

// Example of persistent texture storage

```
GLuint texture;

glGenTextures(1, &texture);

glBindTexture(GL_TEXTURE_2D, texture);

glTexStorage2D(GL_TEXTURE_2D,                levels,
internalFormat, width, height);

glTextureStorage2D(texture,    levels,    internalFormat,
width, height, GL_MAP_PERSISTENT_BIT);
```

1. **Buffer Orphaning:** Another technique for achieving memory persistence is buffer orphaning. By orphaning a buffer (i.e., creating a new buffer object), you can ensure

that data persists in GPU memory even if the buffer is reallocated.

```cpp
// Example of buffer orphaning

GLuint buffer;

glGenBuffers(1, &buffer);

glBindBuffer(GL_ARRAY_BUFFER, buffer);

glBufferData(GL_ARRAY_BUFFER, size, nullptr, GL_STREAM_DRAW);

void* data = glMapBufferRange(GL_ARRAY_BUFFER, 0, size, GL_MAP_WRITE_BIT);

// Fill data buffer

glUnmapBuffer(GL_ARRAY_BUFFER);
```

Conclusion

Direct Memory Access and memory persistence are advanced GPU techniques that can significantly improve data transfer efficiency and memory management in OpenGL applications. Leveraging these techniques allows you to reduce CPU overhead, achieve faster data transfers, and maintain data in GPU memory as needed, ultimately enhancing the performance and responsiveness of your graphics software. In the following sections, we will explore more advanced GPU techniques and programming practices.

Section 2.4: Multi-GPU Programming

Multi-GPU programming is an advanced technique that allows you to harness the power of multiple graphics processing units (GPUs) in a single system to improve the performance of your OpenGL applications. In this section, we will explore the concept of multi-GPU programming, its benefits, and considerations when implementing it.

Understanding Multi-GPU Systems

Modern systems often come equipped with multiple GPUs, either as separate graphics cards or as part of integrated GPU solutions. Multi-GPU programming allows you to distribute rendering workloads across these GPUs, effectively parallelizing rendering tasks and potentially achieving significant performance gains.

Benefits of Multi-GPU Programming

Multi-GPU programming offers several advantages:

1. **Increased Rendering Performance:** By dividing rendering tasks among multiple GPUs, you can achieve higher frame rates and handle more complex scenes in real-time applications.
2. **Enhanced Graphics Quality:** Multi-GPU setups can handle advanced rendering techniques like real-time ray tracing and high-quality global illumination, improving the overall visual quality of your applications.
3. **Improved Compute Performance:** Beyond graphics rendering, multi-GPU systems can accelerate general-purpose computing tasks through GPGPU programming, as discussed in previous sections.

Considerations for Multi-GPU Programming

Implementing multi-GPU programming in OpenGL involves several considerations:

1. **API Support:** OpenGL provides support for multi-GPU configurations through extensions like NVIDIA's NVLink and AMD's CrossFire. Ensure that your target hardware and drivers support these extensions.
2. **Load Balancing:** Efficiently distributing rendering tasks across GPUs is crucial. Consider load-balancing strategies to ensure that each GPU is fully utilized and that tasks are evenly distributed.
3. **Synchronization:** Managing synchronization between GPUs is essential to avoid rendering artifacts. Ensure that rendering commands are synchronized appropriately to maintain consistency in the final frame.
4. **Resource Management:** Managing resources like textures, buffer objects, and shaders across multiple GPUs can be complex. Strategies for resource sharing or duplication may be necessary.

Example Multi-GPU Rendering

Here's a simplified example of how multi-GPU rendering can be achieved in OpenGL:

```
// Initialize OpenGL context on both GPUs (pseudocode)

GPUContext gpu1 = InitializeGPU(1);

GPUContext gpu2 = InitializeGPU(2);

// Load scene data
```

```
LoadSceneData();

while (rendering) {

// Split rendering tasks between GPUs

RenderSceneOnGPU(gpu1);

RenderSceneOnGPU(gpu2);

// Synchronize and composite frames

SynchronizeGPUs(gpu1, gpu2);

CompositeFrames();

// Display the final frame

DisplayFrame();

}
```

Challenges and Considerations

Multi-GPU programming comes with its challenges, including:

- **Complexity:** Multi-GPU programming is more complex than single-GPU programming, requiring careful consideration of synchronization, load balancing, and resource management.

- **Cost:** Multi-GPU setups can be expensive, both in terms of hardware costs and power consumption.

- **Diminishing Returns:** Not all applications benefit equally from multi-GPU setups. Some workloads may see limited performance improvements due to Amdahl's Law limitations.

Conclusion

Multi-GPU programming is an advanced technique that can significantly improve the rendering and compute performance of OpenGL applications. While it offers the potential for higher frame rates and improved graphics quality, it also introduces complexity and considerations for load balancing, synchronization, and resource management. When used effectively, multi-GPU programming can be a powerful tool for optimizing graphics and compute-intensive applications. In the following sections, we will explore more advanced GPU techniques and rendering technologies.

Section 2.5: GPU Culling and LOD

GPU culling and Level of Detail (LOD) techniques are essential for optimizing OpenGL applications by efficiently managing the rendering workload. In this section, we will explore GPU culling and LOD, their significance, and how to implement them effectively.

GPU Culling

GPU culling involves determining which objects or parts of a scene are not visible and can be skipped during rendering. This process helps reduce the rendering workload, improving overall performance. There are several GPU culling techniques, including:

1. **Frustum Culling:** Objects outside the view frustum of the camera are culled. This is a basic technique that quickly eliminates objects not in the camera's field of view.
2. **Occlusion Culling:** Objects hidden behind other objects are culled based on depth or occlusion queries. This

technique reduces overdraw and unnecessary rendering.

3. **Distance Culling:** Objects that are too far from the camera are culled. This is particularly useful for large open-world environments.

4. **LOD Culling:** Objects with different levels of detail (LOD) are used based on their distance from the camera. Distant objects use lower-detail models, reducing rendering complexity.

GPU culling can be implemented using shaders and buffer objects to efficiently discard objects or primitives that are not visible.

Level of Detail (LOD)

Level of Detail (LOD) techniques involve using simplified representations of objects when they are distant from the camera. LOD can significantly reduce rendering workload without sacrificing visual quality. LOD strategies include:

1. **Mesh Simplification:** Generate lower-detail versions of 3D models, such as using fewer polygons, when objects are distant.

2. **Texture Mipmapping:** Use lower-resolution textures for distant objects, reducing memory and bandwidth requirements.

3. **Impostors:** Replace distant objects with 2D images (impostors) that approximate their appearance from a distance.

4. **Billboarding:** Represent objects as 2D billboards (flat sprites) when they are far away, minimizing rendering complexity.

Implementing GPU Culling and LOD

To implement GPU culling and LOD effectively in OpenGL applications:

1. **Shader Programs:** Use shader programs to perform culling and LOD calculations. Frustum culling and distance-based LOD can be implemented in vertex shaders or geometry shaders.
2. **Buffer Objects:** Utilize buffer objects to store culling and LOD information efficiently. For example, you can use buffer objects to store visibility flags or LOD levels for each object.
3. **Compute Shaders:** Compute shaders can be employed for more complex culling and LOD calculations, such as occlusion culling based on ray tracing.
4. **Level of Detail Models:** Prepare a hierarchy of LOD models for each object, from high-detail to low-detail versions. Switch between these models based on the camera's distance to the object.
5. **Texture Management:** Manage texture mipmaps to ensure that distant objects use lower-resolution textures automatically.
6. **Billboarding and Impostors:** Implement techniques like billboarding and impostors for objects like distant trees or vegetation to simplify rendering.

Benefits of GPU Culling and LOD

The benefits of GPU culling and LOD techniques include:

- **Improved Performance:** Reduced rendering workload leads to higher frame rates and smoother gameplay.

- **Efficient Resource Usage:** LOD techniques reduce memory and bandwidth requirements by using lower-detail assets.

- **Scalability:** GPU culling and LOD make applications more scalable, allowing them to run smoothly on a wider range of hardware configurations.

Conclusion

GPU culling and Level of Detail (LOD) techniques are essential tools for optimizing OpenGL applications. They enable efficient management of rendering workloads, leading to improved performance and resource utilization. By implementing these techniques using shaders, buffer objects, and LOD models, you can create visually impressive and efficient graphics applications. In the following sections, we will delve into more advanced graphics optimization techniques and rendering technologies.

Chapter 3: Complex Shader Techniques

Section 3.1: Shader Interpolation Methods

Shader interpolation is a fundamental aspect of modern graphics programming, allowing for smooth transitions of values across vertices and fragments of 3D objects. In this section, we will delve into shader interpolation methods, how they work, and how to utilize them effectively in your OpenGL shaders.

Understanding Shader Interpolation

Shader interpolation, often referred to as "vertex interpolation" or "fragment interpolation," is the process by which values are smoothly interpolated across the vertices and fragments of a rendered object. These values can include colors, normals, texture coordinates, and custom attributes defined in your shaders.

Shader interpolation is crucial for achieving realistic shading effects and smooth transitions between different parts of an object's surface. Without interpolation, objects would appear faceted and unnatural.

Interpolation in the Graphics Pipeline

Shader interpolation occurs at various stages of the graphics pipeline:

1. **Vertex Shader:** Vertex shaders compute values per vertex and pass them to subsequent stages. These values may include vertex positions, normals, and custom attributes.
2. **Rasterization:** During rasterization, the GPU interpolates values between vertices for each fragment within a primitive (e.g., a triangle). This interpolation occurs in

both screen space and normalized device coordinates.

3. **Fragment Shader:** Fragment shaders receive the interpolated values for each fragment. These interpolated values can be used for shading calculations, texture sampling, and other rendering operations.

Interpolation Methods

The most common interpolation method used in shaders is linear interpolation, also known as barycentric interpolation. This method computes interpolated values as weighted averages of the values at the vertices. For example, when interpolating a color, each channel (e.g., red, green, blue) is linearly interpolated separately.

In GLSL, you can access interpolated values in the fragment shader using smooth qualifiers. For example:

in vec3 vertexColor; // *Interpolated color from the vertex shader*

void main() {

// *Use the interpolated color for shading*

gl_FragColor = vec4(vertexColor, 1.0);

}

Custom Interpolation

In some cases, you may want to customize the interpolation method or perform non-linear interpolations. You can achieve this by defining your own interpolation functions in the fragment shader. For instance, you can perform smoothstep interpolation to create smooth transitions:

in vec2 customValue; // *Custom attribute from the vertex shader*

```
void main() {

// Perform smoothstep interpolation

float t = smoothstep(0.0, 1.0, customValue.x);

gl_FragColor = vec4(t, 1.0 - t, 0.0, 1.0); // Transition from red to green

}
```

Conclusion

Shader interpolation is a fundamental aspect of modern graphics programming, enabling smooth transitions of values across vertices and fragments. Understanding how interpolation works in the graphics pipeline and utilizing it effectively in your shaders is essential for creating visually appealing and realistic 3D graphics. In the following sections, we will explore more advanced shader techniques, including stochastic shading and real-time ray tracing.

Section 3.2: Stochastic Shading

Stochastic shading is an advanced shading technique used in computer graphics to introduce controlled randomness into the rendering process. It is particularly useful for achieving more realistic and natural-looking materials and lighting effects. In this section, we will explore the concept of stochastic shading, its applications, and how to implement it in OpenGL shaders.

Understanding Stochastic Shading

Stochastic shading, also known as random sampling or stochastic sampling, is a technique that adds controlled randomness to the shading calculations for individual pixels or fragments. This randomness can mimic real-world imperfections and variations in materials and lighting.

The key idea behind stochastic shading is to introduce randomness into the shading process while ensuring that the randomness is statistically consistent across multiple frames. This consistency helps to prevent flickering or overly noisy results.

Applications of Stochastic Shading

Stochastic shading finds applications in various aspects of computer graphics, including:

1. **Realistic Materials:** Stochastic shading can be used to simulate microsurface imperfections, roughness, and variations in material properties. This adds realism to materials like metals, plastics, and fabrics.
2. **Natural Lighting:** In natural environments, lighting conditions are rarely perfectly uniform. Stochastic shading can introduce subtle variations in lighting, creating more visually interesting and believable scenes.
3. **Anti-Aliasing:** Stochastic sampling can be employed to reduce aliasing artifacts, such as the "jagged" edges seen in computer graphics. By introducing randomness in pixel sampling patterns, aliasing can be mitigated.
4. **Effects like Noise and Grain:** Stochastic shading can be used to simulate effects like film grain, noise, and speckles, which are common in photography and cinematography.

Implementing Stochastic Shading

To implement stochastic shading in OpenGL shaders, you can follow these general steps:

1. **Generate Random Numbers:** Use a pseudorandom number generator (PRNG) to generate random values within a specific range. In GLSL, you can use built-in functions like rand() and fract() for this purpose.
2. **Apply Randomness:** Introduce randomness into various aspects of shading calculations. This can include perturbing surface normals, varying reflection or refraction directions, or adding noise to textures.
3. **Temporal Coherence:** To ensure consistency across frames, use a deterministic PRNG seed. You can pass a frame-specific seed to your shaders to maintain coherence while allowing for variation between frames.

Here's a simple example of adding stochastic shading to simulate roughness in a material's reflection:

```
// Vertex Shader

out vec3 normal;

out vec3 viewDirection;

void main() {

// Calculate normal and view direction as usual

// ...

// Pass them to the fragment shader

normal = normalize(normalMatrix * normal);

viewDirection = normalize(-vPosition);

// ...

}
```

```glsl
// Fragment Shader

in vec3 normal;

in vec3 viewDirection;

uniform float roughness;

uniform float seed; // Frame-specific seed

float rand(vec2 co) {

return fract(sin(dot(co.xy, vec2(12.9898, 78.233))) * 43758.5453);

}

void main() {

// Add stochastic shading for roughness

float random = rand(gl_FragCoord.xy + seed);

vec3 perturbedNormal = normalize(normal + roughness * (random
* 2.0 - 1.0));

// Perform shading using perturbed normal

// ...

gl_FragColor = /* Final shaded color */;

}
```

Benefits of Stochastic Shading

Stochastic shading offers several benefits in computer graphics:

- **Realism:** By introducing controlled randomness, stochastic shading can make materials and lighting appear more natural and realistic.

- **Anti-Aliasing:** Stochastic sampling can help reduce aliasing artifacts, improving overall image quality.

- **Visual Variety:** Stochastic shading can add visual variety to scenes, making them more visually appealing and less predictable.

- **Artistic Control:** Artists and developers have control over the degree and type of randomness applied, allowing for creative and artistic choices.

Conclusion

Stochastic shading is a valuable technique in computer graphics for adding controlled randomness to shading calculations. It finds applications in creating realistic materials, simulating natural lighting variations, reducing aliasing artifacts, and adding visual interest to scenes. When implemented effectively, stochastic shading can enhance the overall quality and realism of computer-generated imagery. In the following sections, we will explore more advanced shader techniques and rendering technologies.

Section 3.3: Real-time Ray Tracing

Real-time ray tracing is a groundbreaking rendering technique that simulates the behavior of light rays in a 3D environment in real-time. Unlike traditional rasterization, which approximates lighting and shadows, ray tracing computes realistic lighting interactions. In this section, we will explore real-time ray tracing, its applications, and how to implement it in OpenGL using modern hardware-accelerated techniques.

Understanding Ray Tracing

Ray tracing is a rendering technique based on the physics of light. It simulates how rays of light interact with objects in a 3D scene, tracing each ray's path as it bounces, reflects, refracts, and ultimately contributes to the final image. This approach enables highly accurate and physically plausible rendering, producing realistic global illumination, shadows, reflections, and refractions.

Traditionally, ray tracing was computationally expensive and primarily used for offline rendering in film and animation. However, recent advances in hardware, including dedicated ray tracing cores in modern GPUs, have made real-time ray tracing feasible for interactive applications.

Ray Tracing in the Graphics Pipeline

Real-time ray tracing is integrated into the graphics pipeline alongside traditional rasterization. The main components of a real-time ray tracing pipeline include:

1. **Ray Generation:** Rays are generated from the camera's viewpoint, typically in the fragment shader. Each ray represents a path that may intersect objects in the scene.
2. **Intersection Testing:** Rays are tested for intersection with scene objects (e.g., triangles or bounding volumes). Modern GPUs use hardware acceleration structures like BVHs (Bounding Volume Hierarchies) to accelerate this process.
3. **Shading:** For each ray-object intersection, shading calculations are performed. This includes computing

lighting, material properties, and determining the color of the pixel.

4. **Ray Tracing Effects:** Real-time ray tracing enables effects like accurate reflections, refractions (transparent materials), global illumination (indirect lighting), and soft shadows, which were challenging to achieve with rasterization alone.

Implementing Real-time Ray Tracing

To implement real-time ray tracing in OpenGL, you can use extensions like NVIDIA's RTX or Vulkan extensions that provide ray tracing capabilities. Here is a simplified overview of how real-time ray tracing is implemented:

1. **Ray Tracing Pipeline Setup:** Configure a ray tracing pipeline with shaders for ray generation, intersection, and shading.
2. **Acceleration Structures:** Build acceleration structures (e.g., BVHs) to optimize ray-object intersection tests.
3. **Shader Programs:** Implement ray generation, intersection, and shading shaders. These shaders define how rays are generated, how intersections are tested, and how shading calculations are performed.
4. **Trace Rays:** In the fragment shader, launch rays for each pixel and trace their paths through the scene. Use the acceleration structures to efficiently find intersections.
5. **Shading and Accumulation:** For each ray-object intersection, perform shading calculations and accumulate the contributions to the final pixel color.
6. **Effects:** Implement ray tracing effects like reflections and refractions by recursively tracing additional rays.

Here is a simplified example of a ray generation shader in GLSL:

```glsl
#version 460

layout(location = 0) buffer image2D {

writeonly layout(binding = 0, rgba8) image2D outputImage;

};

void main() {

// Calculate ray direction based on screen coordinates

vec2 screenCoord = gl_FragCoord.xy;

vec3 rayDirection = /* Compute ray direction based on screenCoord */;

// Perform ray tracing calculations and shading here

// Write the resulting color to the output image

imageStore(outputImage, ivec2(screenCoord), vec4(/* final color */));

}
```

Benefits and Challenges

Real-time ray tracing offers several benefits:

- **Realism:** It produces highly realistic lighting, shadows, and reflections, enhancing the visual quality of interactive applications.

- **Simplified Workflows:** Ray tracing simplifies complex lighting scenarios that traditionally required multiple techniques.

- **Artistic Freedom:** Artists can achieve more natural and artistic lighting effects.

However, real-time ray tracing also poses challenges:

- **Computational Intensity:** Real-time ray tracing is computationally intensive, demanding powerful hardware.

- **Integration Complexity:** Implementing ray tracing alongside rasterization can be complex.

- **Development Resources:** Developing ray-traced applications requires specialized knowledge and tools.

Conclusion

Real-time ray tracing is a revolutionary rendering technique that brings unparalleled realism to interactive graphics applications. With advancements in hardware support and the availability of ray tracing extensions for OpenGL and Vulkan, developers can now harness the power of ray tracing to create visually stunning and physically accurate 3D scenes in real-time. In the following sections, we will explore more advanced rendering techniques and shader effects.

Section 3.4: Subsurface Scattering Implementation

Subsurface scattering (SSS) is a rendering technique used to simulate the behavior of light as it enters and scatters within translucent materials like skin, wax, and certain types of organic materials. SSS is crucial for achieving realistic and believable skin rendering in character models and other organic objects. In this section, we will explore the concept of subsurface scattering, its significance, and how to implement it in OpenGL shaders.

Understanding Subsurface Scattering

Subsurface scattering occurs when light enters a translucent material, scatters within it, and eventually exits at a different point. This phenomenon gives materials like human skin their characteristic soft and warm appearance. Without SSS, skin can appear unnaturally opaque and flat.

SSS is particularly important for achieving realistic skin shading in computer graphics. It simulates the diffusion of light through multiple layers of skin, each with different optical properties. The result is a more lifelike rendering of skin that captures the softness and warmth of real skin.

Subsurface Scattering Models

There are various mathematical models for simulating subsurface scattering, including:

1. **Dipole Approximation:** The dipole model is a simple and widely used approximation for SSS. It assumes that light scatters within a material as if it were absorbed and re-emitted by dipoles (pairs of positive and negative charges).
2. **BSSRDF (Bidirectional Surface Scattering Reflectance Distribution Function):** BSSRDF models provide a more physically accurate representation of SSS by considering the scattering behavior at each point on the surface. These models are computationally intensive but yield highly realistic results.
3. **Diffusion Approximation:** The diffusion approximation simplifies SSS into a diffusion equation that can be solved

efficiently. It provides a good balance between realism and performance.

Implementing Subsurface Scattering

To implement subsurface scattering in OpenGL shaders, you can follow these general steps:

1. **Material Properties:** Define material properties that describe the scattering behavior of the object. This may include parameters like the scattering coefficient, absorption coefficient, and the phase function.
2. **Scattering Calculation:** In the fragment shader, calculate the amount of light that scatters within the material. This involves solving the diffusion equation or using a simplified model like the dipole approximation.
3. **Integration:** Integrate the scattered light over the depth of the material. This typically requires multiple iterations, with each iteration approximating light transport at a different depth.
4. **Shading:** Combine the scattered light with other shading components, such as diffuse and specular reflections, to obtain the final shading result.

Here is a simplified example of SSS implementation using the dipole approximation in GLSL:

```glsl
#version 460

// Material properties

uniform vec3 scatteringColor;

uniform float scatteringCoefficient;
```

```
// Other shader inputs (e.g., normal, view direction, light direction)

void main() {

// Calculate SSS using the dipole approximation

// ...

// Combine SSS with other shading components

vec3 finalColor = /* Combine SSS with diffuse and specular shading
*/;

// Output the final color

gl_FragColor = vec4(finalColor, 1.0);

}
```

Benefits and Challenges

Subsurface scattering offers several benefits in computer graphics:

- **Realism:** SSS enhances the realism of materials like skin, wax, and fruits by simulating light scattering.

- **Believable Skin:** It is crucial for creating believable human skin in character models.

- **Artistic Control:** Artists can adjust material properties to achieve different SSS effects.

However, implementing SSS can be challenging:

- **Computational Cost:** SSS calculations can be computationally expensive, especially with more accurate models like BSSRDF.

- **Parameter Tuning:** Achieving the desired SSS effect often requires fine-tuning of material properties.

- **Integration Complexity:** Integrating SSS into existing shaders can be complex.

Conclusion

Subsurface scattering is a critical rendering technique for achieving realistic and believable materials in computer graphics, especially for simulating skin and organic objects. By understanding the principles of SSS and implementing it in shaders using appropriate models, developers and artists can create visually stunning and lifelike 3D scenes. In the following sections, we will delve into more advanced rendering techniques and graphics technologies.

Section 3.5: Real-time Global Illumination Techniques

Real-time global illumination (GI) is a rendering technique used to simulate indirect lighting interactions between surfaces in a 3D scene. It plays a crucial role in achieving realistic and visually appealing lighting in interactive applications and games. In this section, we will explore real-time global illumination, its significance, and how to implement it in OpenGL shaders.

Understanding Global Illumination

Global illumination refers to the complex interplay of indirect lighting in a scene, where light not only directly illuminates surfaces but also bounces off surfaces and contributes to the illumination of other surfaces. This includes effects like color bleeding, soft shadows, and realistic ambient lighting.

Global illumination is essential for creating scenes that look physically accurate and cohesive. Without it, scenes may appear flat and lack the subtle interplay of light and shadow that occurs in the real world.

Global Illumination Techniques

There are various techniques for achieving real-time global illumination in computer graphics, including:

1. **Screen-Space Reflections (SSR):** SSR techniques trace rays in screen space to approximate reflections and indirect lighting. While efficient, SSR has limitations and may not capture all global illumination effects accurately.
2. **Radiosity:** Radiosity methods simulate global illumination by solving the radiative transfer equation. This technique can produce highly realistic results but can be computationally expensive.
3. **Voxel Cone Tracing:** Voxel cone tracing is a technique that involves representing the 3D scene as a voxel grid. It traces cones of rays from each pixel and samples the voxels to calculate indirect lighting.
4. **Light Propagation Volumes (LPV):** LPV techniques involve storing light information in volumes and propagating it through the scene. This approach is suitable for dynamic scenes and can handle multiple bounces of indirect lighting.
5. **Screen-Space Global Illumination (SSGI):** SSGI combines screen-space techniques with ambient occlusion to approximate global illumination effects efficiently.

Implementing Real-time Global Illumination

Implementing real-time global illumination in OpenGL shaders requires a combination of techniques, depending on the desired level of realism and performance. Here are some general steps to implement SSGI, a screen-space technique, as an example:

1. **G-Buffer:** Render a G-buffer containing information like surface normals, positions, and albedo.
2. **SSGI Pass:** In a separate shader pass, perform screen-space ray tracing or cone tracing to estimate indirect lighting. Use the G-buffer data to guide the tracing.
3. **Ambient Occlusion:** Combine ambient occlusion with the indirect lighting estimation to enhance the global illumination effect.
4. **Shading Integration:** Integrate the indirect lighting with the direct lighting (e.g., from point lights or directional lights) and apply it to the final shading of objects.

Here is a simplified example of a shader pass that performs SSGI:

```glsl
#version 460

uniform sampler2D gBufferNormal;

uniform sampler2D gBufferPosition;

uniform sampler2D gBufferAlbedo;

// Other shader inputs (e.g., screen coordinates)

void main() {

// Read G-buffer data

vec3 normal = texture(gBufferNormal, screenCoord).xyz;
```

```
vec3 position = texture(gBufferPosition, screenCoord).xyz;

vec3 albedo = texture(gBufferAlbedo, screenCoord).xyz;

// Perform SSGI calculations

// ...

// Combine SSGI with direct lighting and apply it to shading

vec3 finalColor = /* Combine SSGI with direct lighting and apply it
to shading */;

// Output the final color

gl_FragColor = vec4(finalColor, 1.0);

}
```

Benefits and Challenges

Real-time global illumination offers several benefits:

- **Realism:** GI enhances realism by simulating complex lighting interactions in scenes.

- **Atmosphere:** It helps create atmospheric and cohesive lighting environments.

- **Visual Appeal:** GI contributes to the visual appeal of scenes, making them more engaging.

However, implementing real-time global illumination has challenges:

- **Performance:** GI calculations can be computationally intensive, demanding powerful hardware or optimizations.

- **Artifacts:** Achieving artifact-free GI can be challenging, and techniques like SSGI may produce occasional visual artifacts.

- **Integration Complexity:** Integrating GI into existing rendering pipelines can be complex.

Conclusion

Real-time global illumination is a critical rendering technique for achieving realistic and visually appealing lighting in interactive applications and games. By understanding the principles of GI and implementing it in shaders using appropriate techniques, developers can create immersive and visually stunning 3D scenes. In the following sections, we will explore more advanced rendering techniques and graphics technologies.

Chapter 4: Deep Learning in Graphics

Section 4.1: Neural Networks for Procedural Content

Neural networks have revolutionized various fields, and their application in computer graphics has led to exciting developments. In this section, we will explore how neural networks are used for generating procedural content, such as textures, models, and even entire game levels.

Procedural Content Generation

Procedural content generation (PCG) is the creation of game content using algorithms rather than manually designing every element. This approach offers several advantages, including reduced development time, smaller file sizes, and the ability to generate vast and diverse game worlds.

Traditionally, PCG algorithms were rule-based, relying on predefined algorithms and parameters to generate content. Neural networks, however, provide a more data-driven and flexible approach to PCG.

Texture Synthesis

One of the most compelling applications of neural networks in procedural content generation is texture synthesis. Neural networks, particularly convolutional neural networks (CNNs), have demonstrated remarkable capabilities in generating realistic textures from scratch or by imitating existing ones.

The process typically involves training a neural network on a dataset of textures. The network learns the statistical properties of textures, such as color patterns, structures, and fine details. Once trained, the network can generate new textures that share similar characteristics.

Here's a simplified example of texture synthesis using a trained neural network:

 # Load a pre-trained neural network for texture synthesis

model = load_texture_synthesis_model()

 # Generate a new texture

new_texture = model.generate_texture()

Procedural Model Generation

Neural networks can also be used to generate 3D models procedurally. For instance, generative adversarial networks (GANs) can be trained to produce 3D models of objects, characters, or environments.

The training process involves feeding the GAN with a dataset of 3D models and training it to generate similar models. Once trained, the GAN can generate new 3D models that resemble the ones it was trained on.

 # Train a GAN for 3D model generation

model = train_3d_model_generation_gan()

 # Generate a new 3D model

new_model = model.generate_model()

Procedural Level Design

In game development, procedural level generation is an area where neural networks can shine. By training a neural network on existing game levels, it can learn the layout, aesthetics, and challenges of those levels. Subsequently, it can generate new levels that are fun, engaging, and coherent.

This approach is particularly useful in creating replayable games with endless variations in level design.

```
# Train a neural network for procedural level generation

model = train_procedural_level_generation_network()

# Generate a new game level

new_level = model.generate_level()
```

Challenges and Considerations

While neural networks offer exciting possibilities for procedural content generation, there are challenges to be aware of:

- **Training Data:** The quality and diversity of training data significantly impact the generated content's quality. Insufficient or biased training data can lead to suboptimal results.

- **Model Complexity:** Training and using neural networks for content generation may require substantial computational resources.

- **Artistic Direction:** Neural networks may struggle to capture the artistic intent of human designers, resulting in a need for post-processing and artistic refinement.

Conclusion

Neural networks are a powerful tool for procedural content generation in computer graphics. Whether used for generating textures, 3D models, or game levels, they open up new creative possibilities and streamline the content creation process. As the field of deep learning continues to advance, we can expect even more exciting applications of neural networks in graphics and game development. In the following sections, we will explore additional ways in which deep learning is transforming the graphics industry.

Section 4.2: Style Transfer in Real-time Rendering

Style transfer is a fascinating application of deep learning that allows us to apply the artistic style of one image to the content of another. In the context of real-time rendering, style transfer techniques enable us to create visually appealing and unique rendering styles for games, simulations, and interactive experiences. In this section, we will explore style transfer in real-time rendering, its significance, and how to implement it using deep learning.

Understanding Style Transfer

Style transfer, at its core, involves two main components: content and style. The content refers to the underlying structure of an image, while the style represents its artistic characteristics, such as brush strokes, color palettes, and textures.

Neural networks, especially convolutional neural networks (CNNs), have shown remarkable abilities in separating content from style in images. This separation allows us to transfer the style of one image onto the content of another, resulting in a new image that combines the content of one source with the artistic style of another.

Real-time Style Transfer

Real-time style transfer is the application of style transfer techniques to the field of real-time rendering, where high frame rates and interactive responsiveness are crucial. This approach enables dynamic and interactive applications, such as games and simulations, to change their rendering style on the fly.

To achieve real-time style transfer, developers can employ pre-trained deep learning models or build custom models tailored to their specific rendering needs.

Implementing Real-time Style Transfer

Implementing real-time style transfer involves several key steps:

1. **Selecting Content and Style Images:** Choose the source content image (e.g., a scene from your game) and the style image (e.g., a famous painting or an artistic rendering).
2. **Pre-processing Images:** Pre-process the content and style images to make them suitable for input into a neural network. This may involve resizing, normalizing, and converting them into a format compatible with the model.
3. **Using a Neural Network Model:** Utilize a pre-trained neural network model designed for style transfer, such as VGG-19 or a custom model. The model should have separate layers to capture content and style features.
4. **Feature Extraction:** Pass the content and style images through the model to extract their content and style features at different layers. These features represent the high-level structure and artistic characteristics.
5. **Optimization:** Create a new image (often referred to as the target image) and initialize it with the content image. Then, iteratively adjust the target image to minimize the

difference between its content and style features and those of the content and style images, respectively.

6. **Rendering Loop:** Integrate the style transfer process into your rendering loop to continuously update the rendering style in real-time.

Here's a simplified example of real-time style transfer using Python and TensorFlow:

```python
# Load pre-trained VGG-19 model

model = load_pretrained_vgg19()

# Define content and style images

content_image = load_content_image()

style_image = load_style_image()

# Extract content and style features

content_features = model(content_image)

style_features = model(style_image)

# Initialize target image with content image

target_image = content_image.clone()

# Optimization loop

for step in range(num_iterations):

# Calculate content and style loss

content_loss        =        calculate_content_loss(target_image, content_features)
```

```
style_loss = calculate_style_loss(target_image, style_features)

# Total loss is a combination of content and style loss

total_loss = content_weight * content_loss + style_weight * style_loss

# Update the target image to minimize the total loss

update_target_image(target_image, total_loss)

# Render the final target image

render(target_image)
```

Benefits and Challenges

Real-time style transfer offers several benefits in real-time rendering:

- **Artistic Freedom:** It allows developers to create unique and visually appealing rendering styles for games and interactive experiences.

- **Dynamic Style Changes:** Real-time style transfer enables dynamic changes in rendering styles during gameplay, enhancing immersion and aesthetics.

- **Highly Interactive:** With optimizations, it can achieve real-time frame rates, making it suitable for interactive applications.

However, there are challenges to consider:

- **Computational Intensity:** Style transfer can be computationally intensive, especially with large neural network models.

- **Parameter Tuning:** Achieving the desired artistic style may require fine-tuning of parameters and hyperparameters.

- **Memory Usage:** Storing and manipulating large neural network models and images can consume significant memory.

Conclusion

Real-time style transfer is a captivating application of deep learning in the field of real-time rendering. By seamlessly blending the content and style of images, it opens up exciting possibilities for creating visually stunning and dynamic rendering styles in games, simulations, and interactive experiences. As real-time rendering technology continues to advance, we can expect even more creative and immersive applications of style transfer in the graphics industry. In the following sections, we will delve into additional ways in which deep learning is transforming graphics and animation.

Section 4.3: AI-driven Animation

AI-driven animation is a groundbreaking application of artificial intelligence in the field of computer graphics. It involves using neural networks and machine learning techniques to generate and enhance animations, making the process more efficient and producing realistic and expressive results. In this section, we will explore AI-driven animation, its significance, and its various applications.

Animation Generation

Traditional animation techniques often involve time-consuming manual keyframing, where animators specify the position, rotation, and scale of objects in each frame. AI-driven animation, on the other hand, automates and enhances this process by leveraging neural networks and machine learning models.

These models can generate animations based on input data, such as character movements, facial expressions, or even natural language descriptions. This significantly speeds up the animation production pipeline and allows animators to focus on creative aspects.

Facial Animation

One of the most prominent applications of AI-driven animation is facial animation. AI algorithms can analyze audio and video inputs to generate realistic lip syncing and facial expressions for characters in real-time. This technology has found extensive use in gaming, film production, and virtual communication.

For example, an AI-driven facial animation system can analyze a person's speech and generate corresponding lip movements and facial expressions for an animated character, ensuring that it appears to speak and emote naturally.

```
# Example code for real-time facial animation using AI

def generate_facial_animation(audio_input):

# Use AI model to generate lip movements and facial expressions

facial_animation = ai_model.generate_facial_animation(audio_input)

# Apply the generated animation to the character model

character_model.apply_facial_animation(facial_animation)

# Render the animated character

render(character_model)
```

Motion Capture and Pose Estimation

AI-driven animation is also utilized in motion capture and pose estimation. Machine learning models can analyze video footage or sensor data to accurately track the movements of actors or objects and then apply these movements to 3D character models or animations.

For example, a motion capture system powered by AI can capture the movements of a dancer and map them to a virtual character in real-time, creating a realistic and expressive dance animation.

Procedural Animation

AI can generate procedural animations based on predefined rules and learned behaviors. This is particularly useful for creating natural and lifelike animations for characters and creatures in games and simulations.

For instance, an AI-driven procedural animation system can simulate the locomotion of animals or the behavior of NPCs in a game world, making them respond realistically to the environment and player interactions.

```python
# Example code for procedural animation using AI

def generate_procedural_animation(character_model, ai_behavior):

    # Use AI to generate procedural animation based on behavior

    procedural_animation = ai_model.generate_procedural_animation(ai_behavior)

    # Apply the procedural animation to the character model
```

character_model.apply_procedural_animation(procedural_animation)

 # Render the animated character

render(character_model)

Challenges and Considerations

While AI-driven animation offers numerous advantages, there are challenges to consider:

- **Data Quality:** The quality and diversity of training data can significantly impact the realism of AI-driven animations. High-quality data and diverse training scenarios are crucial.

- **Complexity:** Developing and fine-tuning AI models for animation can be complex and resource-intensive.

- **Artistic Control:** AI-driven animations may require post-processing and artistic refinement to align with the creative vision.

- **Hardware Requirements:** Real-time AI-driven animation often demands powerful hardware, especially for complex models.

Conclusion

AI-driven animation is a transformative technology in computer graphics that enhances the animation production process and enables the creation of more realistic and expressive animations. Whether it's facial animation, motion capture, procedural animation, or other applications, AI is revolutionizing the way animations are created in games, films, and various interactive media.

As AI and machine learning continue to advance, we can expect even more sophisticated and creative applications in the realm of computer-generated animation. In the following sections, we will explore additional areas where AI is shaping the graphics and gaming industries.

Section 4.4: Neural Networks in Texture Generation

Neural networks have gained prominence in the field of texture generation, offering a powerful approach to creating realistic and high-quality textures for various applications, including gaming, 3D modeling, and computer graphics. In this section, we will explore how neural networks are used in texture generation, their significance, and implementation techniques.

Texture Synthesis

Texture synthesis is the process of creating textures that exhibit specific visual characteristics, such as patterns, colors, and details. Traditional texture synthesis methods often involve manually designing textures or using procedural algorithms. However, neural networks have introduced a data-driven and more efficient approach to texture synthesis.

Neural networks, particularly convolutional neural networks (CNNs), can learn the statistical properties of textures from large datasets. These networks can then generate new textures that share similar statistical characteristics, making them visually convincing and coherent.

Neural Style Transfer

Neural style transfer, introduced in a previous section, is also applicable to texture generation. By separating content and style from an input image, neural networks can generate textures that combine the content of one image with the artistic style of another.

This technique is particularly useful for creating textures with specific artistic styles or emulating the appearance of textures found in artwork or photographs.

```
# Example code for texture generation using neural style transfer

def generate_texture(content_image, style_image):

# Use a neural network model for style transfer

generated_texture    =    neural_style_transfer(content_image, style_image)

# Render the generated texture

render(generated_texture)
```

Super-Resolution and Detail Enhancement

Neural networks can enhance the level of detail and resolution in textures. This is crucial for applications like upscaling low-resolution textures in real-time rendering or improving the quality of textures in 3D modeling.

Generative adversarial networks (GANs) are commonly used for super-resolution tasks. These networks can generate high-resolution textures by learning the relationship between low-resolution inputs and their corresponding high-resolution counterparts.

```
# Example code for texture super-resolution using GANs
```

```python
def enhance_texture(low_resolution_texture):

# Use a GAN model for texture super-resolution

high_resolution_texture                                          =
gan_super_resolution(low_resolution_texture)

# Render the enhanced texture

render(high_resolution_texture)
```

Texture Style Transfer

Texture style transfer is an extension of neural style transfer that focuses specifically on transferring the style of one texture to another. This technique allows for the creation of textures that exhibit the visual characteristics of different styles while preserving the underlying content.

Texture style transfer is valuable for artists and designers who want to explore various texture styles for their projects.

```python
# Example code for texture style transfer

def transfer_texture_style(content_texture, style_texture):

# Use a neural network model for texture style transfer

stylized_texture  =  neural_texture_style_transfer(content_texture,
style_texture)

# Render the stylized texture

render(stylized_texture)
```

Challenges and Considerations

Texture generation using neural networks comes with its set of challenges and considerations:

- **Training Data:** High-quality and diverse training datasets are essential for training neural networks to generate realistic textures.

- **Computational Resources:** Training and using neural networks for texture generation can be computationally intensive, demanding powerful hardware or cloud-based resources.

- **Artistic Control:** While neural networks can generate textures, achieving precise artistic control may require post-processing and artistic refinement.

- **Integration:** Integrating neural network-based texture generation into existing graphics pipelines can be complex.

Conclusion

Neural networks have revolutionized texture generation in computer graphics, providing a data-driven and efficient approach to creating realistic and visually appealing textures. Whether it's texture synthesis, style transfer, super-resolution, or style transfer specific to textures, neural networks offer versatile tools for artists, game developers, and 3D modelers. As the field of deep learning continues to advance, we can expect further innovations in texture generation techniques, enabling even more creative and immersive experiences in the world of computer graphics. In the following sections, we will explore additional applications of AI and deep learning in graphics and animation.

Section 4.5: Advanced AI for Game Logic

Artificial intelligence (AI) plays a fundamental role in shaping the behavior and interactions of non-player characters (NPCs) and entities within video games. While AI has been a staple in game development for decades, recent advancements in deep learning and machine learning have ushered in a new era of advanced AI for game logic. In this section, we will explore the applications, techniques, and significance of advanced AI in game development.

Evolving NPCs

Traditionally, NPCs in games were controlled by rule-based systems or scripted behaviors. Advanced AI techniques now enable NPCs to adapt, learn, and evolve their behavior over time, making games more dynamic and immersive.

Reinforcement learning is one such technique where NPCs learn by trial and error. They receive rewards or penalties based on their actions, allowing them to optimize their behavior. This can result in NPCs that become more skilled at tasks, strategize better, and even develop unique personalities.

```python
# Example code for NPC behavior using reinforcement learning

def train_npc_behavior(npc_agent):
# Use reinforcement learning to train the NPC agent

npc_agent.train()

# Apply the learned behavior to the NPC in the game world
```

apply_learned_behavior_to_npc(npc_agent)

Dynamic Game Worlds

Advanced AI can also be used to create dynamic game worlds that respond to player actions and environmental changes. Procedural generation techniques, coupled with AI, can generate game worlds that adapt in real-time to provide unique and challenging experiences.

For example, an AI-driven ecosystem simulation can model the behavior of creatures and plants in a virtual ecosystem. As players interact with the environment, the AI responds by simulating the consequences of those actions, leading to an ever-changing and realistic game world.

 # Example code for dynamic game world simulation using AI

def simulate_game_world(player_actions):

 # Use AI to simulate the game world and NPCs' responses

game_world.simulate(player_actions)

 # Update the game world based on AI-driven simulations

update_game_world(game_world)

Natural Language Interaction

Advanced AI can enhance player-NPC interactions by enabling natural language understanding and generation. This allows players to communicate with NPCs using text or voice, making dialogues and quests more immersive.

Natural language processing (NLP) techniques enable NPCs to understand and respond to player input, making conversations feel more dynamic and responsive to player choices.

 # Example code for natural language interaction with NPCs

def interact_with_npc(player_input, npc_dialogue_model):

 # Use NLP techniques to process player input and generate NPC responses

npc_response   = npc_dialogue_model.generate_response(player_input)

 # Display the NPC's response in the game dialogue

display_npc_response(npc_response)

AI-Driven Storytelling

AI can also be used to create branching narratives and dynamic storylines in games. By analyzing player choices and behaviors, AI-driven storytelling systems can adapt the game's plot and character interactions, resulting in a personalized and engaging narrative experience.

These systems can model player preferences and craft narratives that resonate with individual players, enhancing the replayability and emotional impact of games.

 # Example code for AI-driven storytelling in games

def adapt_game_storyline(player_choices, story_model):

 # Use AI to adapt the game's storyline based on player choices

updated_storyline = story_model.adapt(player_choices)

 # Display the updated storyline in the game

display_updated_storyline(updated_storyline)

Challenges and Considerations

While advanced AI in game logic offers exciting possibilities, there are challenges to address:

- **Computational Resources:** Implementing advanced AI may require substantial computational power, especially for training neural networks or simulating complex game worlds.

- **Data Quality:** Training AI models for game behavior requires high-quality and diverse training data to ensure realistic and varied responses.

- **Balancing Difficulty:** Balancing game difficulty with AI-controlled NPCs is crucial to provide enjoyable and challenging gameplay experiences.

- **Player Experience:** Care must be taken to ensure that AI-driven interactions enhance rather than detract from the player's experience.

Conclusion

Advanced AI for game logic is transforming the landscape of game development, ushering in a new era of dynamic and immersive gaming experiences. Whether it's evolving NPCs, dynamic game worlds, natural language interactions, or AI-driven storytelling, these techniques are shaping the future of gaming. As AI technologies continue to advance, we can anticipate even more innovative applications that push the boundaries of interactive entertainment. In the following sections, we will explore additional areas where AI and deep learning are influencing graphics, animation, and gaming.

Chapter 5: Advanced Simulation Techniques

Section 5.1: Fluid and Gas Dynamics

Advanced simulation techniques for fluid and gas dynamics are essential components of computer graphics, animation, and scientific visualization. These techniques enable the realistic rendering and animation of phenomena like flowing water, smoke, fire, and atmospheric effects. In this section, we will delve into the fundamentals, applications, and methods used in simulating fluid and gas dynamics.

Fundamentals of Fluid Dynamics

Fluid dynamics is the study of how fluids (liquids and gases) move and interact with their surroundings. In computer graphics, simulating fluid dynamics involves solving the Navier-Stokes equations, which describe the behavior of fluids under various conditions. These equations consider parameters like viscosity, density, and velocity to model fluid flow.

In practical terms, simulating fluid dynamics requires discretizing the fluid domain into a grid, simulating the flow of fluid particles through this grid, and updating properties at each grid cell over time.

```
# Example code for simulating fluid dynamics (simplified)

def simulate_fluid_dynamics(grid, time_step):

for _ in range(num_iterations):

# Calculate velocity and pressure based on Navier-Stokes equations
```

calculate_velocity(grid)

calculate_pressure(grid)

 # Update fluid properties over the grid

update_grid(grid, time_step)

Applications in Computer Graphics

Fluid and gas dynamics simulations find applications in various areas of computer graphics:

- **Realistic Water Simulation:** Simulating water flow, waves, and splashes in games and animations to create realistic water bodies like oceans, rivers, and lakes.

- **Fire and Smoke Effects:** Generating convincing fire and smoke animations for special effects in movies, games, and simulations.

- **Atmospheric Effects:** Simulating atmospheric phenomena like clouds, wind, and fog to enhance the realism of outdoor scenes.

- **Particle Systems:** Integrating fluid dynamics into particle systems for dynamic and interactive effects like sand, dust, and snow.

Computational Challenges

Simulating fluid and gas dynamics is computationally demanding due to the complexity of the Navier-Stokes equations and the need for high spatial and temporal resolutions. Achieving real-time simulations often requires optimizations and parallel computing.

Additionally, simulating interactions between fluids and solid objects, such as fluid flowing around obstacles, adds further computational complexity.

Numerical Methods

Several numerical methods are used to solve the Navier-Stokes equations, including finite difference, finite volume, and finite element methods. These methods discretize the fluid domain into grids or elements and update fluid properties iteratively.

In recent years, techniques like smoothed-particle hydrodynamics (SPH) and lattice Boltzmann methods have gained popularity for simulating fluids in computer graphics due to their ability to handle complex fluid behaviors and adapt to varying grid resolutions.

Conclusion

Fluid and gas dynamics simulations are pivotal in computer graphics, animation, and scientific visualization. These simulations enable the creation of stunning visual effects, enhance realism in virtual environments, and contribute to our understanding of real-world fluid phenomena. As computational power continues to grow and simulation methods advance, we can anticipate even more lifelike and interactive fluid and gas simulations in future graphics and animation applications. In the following sections, we will explore other advanced simulation techniques in the realm of computer graphics.

Section 5.2: Rigid Body Dynamics

Rigid body dynamics is a fundamental simulation technique in computer graphics and physics simulations. It deals with the motion and interactions of solid objects that do not deform under external forces. In this section, we will explore the principles, applications, and methods involved in simulating rigid body dynamics.

Principles of Rigid Body Dynamics

At the core of rigid body dynamics is Newton's laws of motion, which govern the behavior of objects under the influence of forces. Rigid bodies are characterized by their mass, shape, and orientation, and their motion is determined by the sum of external forces acting on them.

The equations of motion for rigid bodies account for translational motion (linear movement) and rotational motion (angular movement). These equations are typically expressed in terms of position, velocity, and acceleration.

```
# Example code for rigid body dynamics (simplified)

def simulate_rigid_body(rigid_body, time_step):

    # Calculate forces and torques acting on the rigid body

    calculate_forces(rigid_body)

    calculate_torques(rigid_body)

    # Update position and orientation based on equations of motion

    update_position(rigid_body, time_step)

    update_orientation(rigid_body, time_step)
```

Applications in Computer Graphics

Rigid body dynamics simulations have a wide range of applications in computer graphics and simulations:

- **Physics-based Animation:** Creating realistic movement and collisions of objects in games, films, and virtual simulations.

- **Mechanical Engineering Simulations:** Analyzing and testing the behavior of mechanical components and structures in virtual environments.

- **Robotics:** Simulating the motion and interactions of robot components for control and planning purposes.

- **Vehicle Simulations:** Modeling the dynamics of vehicles, including cars, airplanes, and spacecraft, for flight and driving simulations.

Collision Detection and Response

A crucial aspect of rigid body dynamics is collision detection and response. Detecting when two or more rigid bodies intersect and resolving these collisions accurately is essential for realistic simulations.

Collision detection algorithms check for intersections between object bounding volumes or by examining the geometry of objects themselves. When a collision is detected, collision response algorithms calculate how objects should react, accounting for conservation of momentum and energy.

```python
# Example code for collision detection and response

def detect_and_resolve_collisions(rigid_bodies):

for pair in find_colliding_pairs(rigid_bodies):

# Detect collision between pair of rigid bodies
```

```
collision_point = detect_collision(pair)
```

 # Resolve collision by adjusting velocities and positions

```
resolve_collision(pair, collision_point)
```

Integration Methods

Numerical integration methods are used to advance the simulation over time. Popular methods include the explicit Euler method, semi-implicit Euler method, and Verlet integration. These methods update positions and velocities at discrete time steps based on the equations of motion.

Choosing the right integration method is crucial for stability and accuracy, especially when dealing with fast-moving or highly dynamic simulations.

Challenges and Considerations

Simulating rigid body dynamics can be challenging due to several factors:

- **Complex Interactions:** Objects can collide, slide, roll, and stack on top of each other, leading to intricate interactions.

- **Efficiency:** Handling a large number of rigid bodies or complex geometries can be computationally intensive, requiring optimizations for real-time simulations.

- **Friction and Material Properties:** Modeling friction, restitution (bounciness), and material properties accurately is essential for realistic simulations.

Conclusion

Rigid body dynamics is a foundational technique in computer graphics and simulations that enables the realistic animation and interaction of solid objects. From gaming and films to engineering and robotics, its applications are diverse and far-reaching. Advances in collision detection, integration methods, and hardware acceleration continue to improve the fidelity and performance of rigid body simulations. In the following sections, we will explore additional advanced simulation techniques in computer graphics and animation.

Section 5.3: Soft Body Simulation with Finite Elements

Soft body simulation is a sophisticated technique used in computer graphics to model and animate objects that deform and interact in a physically plausible manner. Unlike rigid bodies, which maintain their shape, soft bodies can bend, stretch, and deform realistically. In this section, we will explore soft body simulation using finite elements, its applications, and the underlying principles.

Finite Element Method

The finite element method (FEM) is a numerical technique used to approximate the behavior of continuous materials by dividing them into discrete elements. In the context of soft body simulation, FEM breaks down deformable objects into a mesh of interconnected elements, such as triangles or tetrahedra. Each element represents a small part of the object.

FEM models the behavior of each element by considering factors like material properties (e.g., elasticity, stiffness), mass, and external forces. By integrating these equations for all elements, FEM calculates the deformation and motion of the entire soft body.

 # Example code for soft body simulation with FEM

def simulate_soft_body(mesh, time_step):

for _ **in** range(num_iterations):

 # Calculate forces and deformations for each finite element

calculate_forces(mesh)

calculate_deformations(mesh)

 # Update the mesh based on the FEM equations of motion

update_mesh(mesh, time_step)

Applications in Computer Graphics

Soft body simulations using finite elements find applications in various areas of computer graphics and animation:

- **Character Animation:** Creating realistic and flexible character models with deformable skin, muscles, and clothing.

- **Physics-based Special Effects:** Simulating deformable objects like balloons, cloth, or jelly-like substances for games, films, and simulations.

- **Medical Visualization:** Modeling and animating biological tissues, organs, and deformations for medical simulations and visualizations.

- **Virtual Surgery:** Simulating soft tissue deformation during surgical procedures for medical training and planning.

Material Models

In soft body simulation, choosing an appropriate material model is crucial for accurately representing the behavior of deformable objects. Common material models include:

- **Linear Elasticity:** Assumes linear deformation behavior under stress and is suitable for modeling materials like rubber and silicone.

- **Neo-Hookean:** Models hyperelastic materials that exhibit nonlinear elasticity, such as biological tissues.

- **St. Venant-Kirchhoff:** Represents an extension of linear elasticity for modeling large deformations.

- **Corotational:** An efficient and accurate model for simulating both linear and nonlinear elastic materials.

The choice of material model depends on the physical properties of the object being simulated and the desired level of realism.

Collision Handling

Collisions between soft bodies and other objects or surfaces need to be handled accurately. Collision detection algorithms identify intersections between the soft body mesh and external objects, while collision response methods determine how the soft body should react, including deformation and rebound.

Efficient collision handling is essential to ensure stable and visually plausible simulations.

```
# Example code for collision handling in soft body simulation

def handle_collisions(mesh, external_objects):

for object in external_objects:

if detect_collision(mesh, object):

# Resolve collision by adjusting deformations and velocities

resolve_collision(mesh, object)
```

Challenges and Considerations

Soft body simulation with finite elements presents several challenges:

- **Computational Complexity:** Handling a large number of elements can be computationally expensive, requiring optimizations for real-time applications.

- **Integration and Stability:** Choosing suitable numerical integration methods and ensuring simulation stability are crucial for accurate results.

- **Parameter Tuning:** Tuning material properties and parameters to match real-world behavior can be time-consuming.

- **Artistic Control:** Balancing realism with artistic control is essential for creating visually appealing deformations.

Conclusion

Soft body simulation with finite elements is a powerful technique that enables the realistic animation and interaction of deformable objects in computer graphics and animation. Whether it's character modeling, special effects, medical simulations, or other applications, this approach offers a versatile tool for creating lifelike and dynamic soft bodies. Advances in numerical methods and hardware acceleration continue to push the boundaries of what can be achieved with soft body simulations. In the following sections, we will explore additional advanced simulation techniques in computer graphics and animation.

Section 5.4: Hair and Fur Simulation

Hair and fur simulation is a vital component of computer graphics, used to create realistic and dynamic representations of hair, fur, feathers, and other fibrous structures. This technique is employed in a wide range of applications, from character animation to animal rendering and special effects. In this section, we will explore the principles, methods, and applications of hair and fur simulation in computer graphics.

Principles of Hair and Fur Simulation

Hair and fur are composed of numerous individual strands that can bend, twist, and interact with one another and their environment. The simulation of hair and fur involves modeling the behavior of these strands based on physical principles such as elasticity, gravity, and friction.

Each hair strand is represented as a series of connected segments or particles. These segments are influenced by external forces, such as wind or collisions, as well as internal forces, like tension and compression within the strand.

 # Example code for simulating hair and fur

def simulate_hair_and_fur(hair_particles, time_step):

for _ **in** range(num_iterations):

 # Calculate external forces (e.g., gravity, wind)

calculate_external_forces(hair_particles)

 # Calculate internal forces (e.g., tension, bending)

calculate_internal_forces(hair_particles)

 # Update positions and orientations of hair particles

update_hair_particles(hair_particles, time_step)

Applications in Computer Graphics

Hair and fur simulation has a wide range of applications in computer graphics:

- **Character Animation:** Creating realistic hair for animated characters, whether it's human hair, animal fur, or stylized hair.

- **Creature Design:** Rendering creatures with intricate fur patterns, such as lions, tigers, and bears.

- **Special Effects:** Generating dynamic fur for special effects, like furry creatures in movies or games.

- **Environmental Effects:** Simulating grass, foliage, and vegetation in outdoor scenes.

Collision Detection and Response

Handling collisions between hair/fur and other objects or surfaces is a crucial aspect of simulation. Collision detection algorithms identify intersections between hair strands and external geometry, while collision response methods determine how hair should react, including bending, sliding, or rebounding.

Efficient collision handling is essential for preventing unrealistic penetrations and ensuring visually plausible results.

 # Example code for collision handling in hair and fur simulation

def handle_collisions(hair_particles, external_geometry):

for object **in** external_geometry:

if detect_collision(hair_particles, object):

 # Resolve collision by adjusting hair positions and orientations

resolve_collision(hair_particles, object)

Dynamics and Styling

In addition to physical simulation, hair and fur systems often include tools for styling and controlling the appearance of the strands. Artists can manipulate parameters like length, curliness, stiffness, and density to achieve the desired look.

Real-time feedback and interactive grooming tools allow artists to create a wide range of styles, from flowing locks to intricate patterns.

 # Example code for interactive hair styling

```
def style_hair(hair_particles, styling_parameters):
    # Apply artist-defined styling parameters to hair particles
    apply_styling(hair_particles, styling_parameters)
```

Challenges and Considerations

Hair and fur simulation presents several challenges:

- **Computational Complexity**: Simulating a large number of hair strands with multiple segments can be computationally demanding, requiring optimization techniques for real-time applications.

- **Collision Handling**: Ensuring accurate collision detection and response while maintaining efficiency is crucial.

- **Realism vs. Performance**: Balancing realism with computational performance is essential to achieve the desired visual quality within time constraints.

- **Artistic Control**: Providing artists with intuitive tools for styling and controlling hair and fur is essential for achieving specific looks.

Conclusion

Hair and fur simulation is a critical technique in computer graphics that enhances the realism and visual appeal of characters, creatures, and scenes. Advances in simulation methods, collision handling, and interactive grooming tools continue to improve the quality and efficiency of hair and fur rendering. As computer graphics technology evolves, we can expect even more impressive and lifelike representations of hair and fur in various applications. In the following sections, we will explore additional advanced simulation techniques in the realm of computer graphics and animation.

Section 5.5: Crowd Dynamics

Crowd dynamics simulation is a fascinating and essential aspect of computer graphics used to replicate the movement and behavior of large groups of individuals, such as crowds at events, pedestrians in urban scenes, or armies in battle simulations. This technique plays a crucial role in creating realistic and immersive virtual environments. In this section, we will delve into the principles, methods, and applications of crowd dynamics simulation in computer graphics.

Principles of Crowd Dynamics

Crowd dynamics simulation is based on the principles of agent-based modeling. It involves modeling individual entities (agents) within a crowd, each with its own behavior and decision-making capabilities. Agents interact with each other and their environment, leading to the emergence of crowd behavior.

Agents' behaviors can range from simple rules, like avoiding collisions or following a path, to more complex decision-making processes, such as social interactions and group formation.

```python
# Example code for simulating crowd dynamics

def simulate_crowd(agents, time_step):

for _ in range(num_iterations):

# Update each agent's behavior based on its surroundings

update_agent_behaviors(agents)
```

 # Apply crowd interaction rules

apply_crowd_interaction(agents)

 # Update agent positions and velocities

update_agent_positions(agents, time_step)

Applications in Computer Graphics

Crowd dynamics simulations have numerous applications in computer graphics and animation:

- **Game Environments:** Creating realistic crowds in video games, enhancing gameplay, and adding immersion to game worlds.

- **Film Production:** Simulating large-scale crowd scenes for movies, historical reenactments, or fantasy settings.

- **Architectural Visualization:** Visualizing how crowds move within and interact with architectural spaces, like stadiums or transportation hubs.

- **Urban Planning:** Analyzing pedestrian flow and behavior in urban environments for city planning and safety assessments.

Crowd Behavior Modeling

Modeling crowd behavior requires defining rules and behaviors for agents. These behaviors can include:

- **Path Following:** Agents following predefined paths or waypoints, such as pedestrians walking on sidewalks or cars following lanes.

- **Obstacle Avoidance:** Agents avoiding collisions with obstacles and other agents to maintain personal space.

- **Social Interactions:** Modeling interactions between agents based on social norms, such as forming groups or queues.

- **Flocking:** Replicating flocking behavior seen in birds or fish, where agents align, separate, and cohere with their neighbors.

```python
# Example code for crowd behavior modeling (flocking)

def update_agent_behaviors(agents):

for agent in agents:

# Calculate forces for alignment, separation, and cohesion

alignment_force = calculate_alignment(agent, neighbors)

separation_force = calculate_separation(agent, neighbors)

cohesion_force = calculate_cohesion(agent, neighbors)

# Apply forces to update agent's velocity

update_agent_velocity(agent, alignment_force, separation_force, cohesion_force)
```

Collision Handling

Handling collisions within a crowd is crucial for realism. Agents need to avoid overlapping with each other or with obstacles in the environment. Collision detection and response algorithms are used to achieve this.

Efficient collision handling is essential, especially when simulating large crowds.

 # Example code for collision handling in crowd dynamics

def handle_collisions(agents, obstacles):

for agent **in** agents:

for obstacle **in** obstacles:

if detect_collision(agent, obstacle):

 # Resolve collision by adjusting agent's position

resolve_collision(agent, obstacle)

Challenges and Considerations

Crowd dynamics simulation comes with several challenges:

- **Scalability:** Simulating large crowds with thousands of agents can be computationally intensive, requiring optimization techniques and parallelization.

- **Realistic Behavior:** Balancing between realism and computational performance is a challenge, as modeling each agent's detailed behavior can be complex.

- **Complex Interactions:** Modeling complex social interactions, such as group formation and leadership, requires sophisticated agent behavior models.

- **Artistic Control:** Providing artists or designers with tools to influence crowd behavior and appearance is crucial for achieving specific visual goals.

Conclusion

Crowd dynamics simulation is a fundamental technique in computer graphics and animation that enables the creation of realistic and immersive crowd scenes in various applications. Advances in agent behavior modeling, collision handling, and hardware acceleration continue to push the boundaries of what can be achieved with crowd simulations. As technology evolves, we can expect even more convincing and dynamic crowd representations in virtual environments. In the following sections, we will explore additional advanced simulation techniques in computer graphics and animation.

Chapter 6: Volumetric and Holographic Rendering

Section 6.1: Introduction to Volumetrics

Volumetric rendering is a technique used in computer graphics to simulate the interaction of light with three-dimensional volumes of data. Unlike traditional surface-based rendering, which focuses on the appearance of object surfaces, volumetric rendering considers the properties of the entire volume. This section introduces the fundamental concepts

Section 6.2: Real-time Volumetric Shadows

Real-time volumetric shadows play a crucial role in enhancing the realism of scenes involving volumetric objects, such as smoke, clouds, or complex lighting effects. These shadows simulate the occlusion of light within volumetric data, adding depth and dimensionality to the rendered scene. In this section, we will explore the concept of real-time volumetric shadows and the techniques used to achieve them.

Understanding Volumetric Shadows

Volumetric shadows are the result of the interaction between light sources and volumetric data. When a light source is obstructed by volumetric objects, it creates shadows within the volume. These shadows are characterized by the attenuation of light intensity, creating regions of lower illumination.

Shadow Mapping for Volumetric Shadows

One common technique for rendering volumetric shadows in real-time is shadow mapping. Shadow mapping involves rendering the scene from the perspective of the light source and storing depth information in a texture known as the shadow map. During the rendering of the main scene, the shadow map is sampled to determine whether a pixel is in shadow.

```
// Example pseudocode for shadow mapping

// Rendering shadow map from light's perspective

for each visible voxel in the volume:

// Transform voxel position to light's view space

vec4 voxelPositionLightSpace = lightProjectionMatrix * lightViewMatrix * vec4(voxelPosition, 1.0);

// Calculate depth from light's perspective

float depth = voxelPositionLightSpace.z / voxelPositionLightSpace.w;

// Store depth in shadow map

shadowMap(depth) = 1.0;

// Rendering the main scene

for each pixel in the frame:

// Transform pixel position to light's view space

vec4 pixelPositionLightSpace = lightProjectionMatrix * lightViewMatrix * vec4(pixelPosition, 1.0);
```

```
// Calculate depth from light's perspective

float depth = pixelPositionLightSpace.z / pixelPositionLightSpace.w;

// Compare depth to shadow map and determine shadow intensity

float shadowIntensity = (depth < shadowMap(depth)) ? 0.0 : 1.0;

// Apply shadow intensity to pixel color

finalColor = objectColor * (1.0 - shadowIntensity);
```

Volumetric Shadow Challenges

Rendering real-time volumetric shadows presents challenges:

- **Sampling and Resolution:** Achieving high-quality shadows requires adequate sampling and resolution of the volumetric data, which can be computationally expensive.

- **Light Scattering:** Simulating light scattering within volumetric media accurately can be complex, especially for multiple scattering events.

- **Performance:** Real-time rendering of volumetric shadows can be demanding, and optimizations are often necessary to maintain interactive frame rates.

- **Integration with Other Techniques:** Integrating volumetric shadows with other rendering techniques, such as global illumination, requires careful consideration.

In practice, real-time volumetric shadows are used in various applications, including games, simulations, and scientific visualization, where they contribute to the visual fidelity of volumetric scenes. Advanced techniques, such as ray marching and precomputed shadow maps, are employed to address the challenges associated with rendering volumetric shadows in real-time.

In the subsequent sections, we will explore additional aspects of volumetric rendering, including holographic displays, volumetric shader techniques, and interactive volumetric data visualization, providing insights into their implementation and applications.

Section 6.3: Holographic Displays and OpenGL

Holographic displays represent an exciting frontier in computer graphics, offering the potential for immersive 3D experiences that extend beyond the limitations of traditional 2D screens. In this section, we will delve into the concept of holographic displays and explore how OpenGL, a widely used graphics API, can be leveraged for rendering holographic content.

Understanding Holographic Displays

Holographic displays differ from conventional displays in that they create images that appear three-dimensional to the viewer, often without the need for specialized eyewear. These displays use various techniques to project light in ways that mimic the behavior of light in the real world, creating the illusion of depth and volume. Holographic displays find applications in fields such as entertainment, medical visualization, design, and education.

Types of Holographic Displays

There are several types of holographic displays, including:

- **Head-up Displays (HUDs):** These displays overlay holographic information onto the viewer's real-world field of view. They are commonly used in augmented reality (AR) applications.

- **Holographic Projection Displays:** These displays use techniques such as spatial light modulation to project 3D holographic content into physical space, allowing viewers to see and interact with 3D objects.

- **Holographic Screens:** These displays are akin to traditional screens but can render 3D holographic content without the need for special glasses or headsets.

OpenGL and Holographic Rendering

OpenGL is a versatile graphics API that can be adapted for rendering content on holographic displays. To leverage OpenGL for holographic rendering, several considerations come into play:

1. Stereoscopic Rendering

Holographic displays often require stereoscopic rendering, where two slightly different views of the scene are presented to each eye to create depth perception. OpenGL can be configured to render stereoscopic views for these displays.

2. Shader Techniques

Shaders are crucial for creating the visual effects needed for holographic displays. This includes techniques for simulating light diffraction, refraction, and interference, which are fundamental to holography.

// Example GLSL shader for simulating holographic interference patterns

void main() {

// Calculate holographic interference effects

// ...

// Output final pixel color

gl_FragColor = finalColor;

}

3. Light Field Rendering

Some holographic displays, particularly light field displays, require rendering not just from specific viewpoints but from a range of viewpoints to create parallax and allow viewers to move around the holographic object.

4. Real-time Interactivity

Interactive holographic applications, such as holographic games or design tools, require real-time rendering and responsiveness. OpenGL can be optimized to meet these requirements.

Challenges in Holographic Rendering

Rendering for holographic displays presents unique challenges:

- **High Computational Demands:** Achieving realistic holographic effects can be computationally intensive, requiring powerful hardware and efficient rendering techniques.

- **Viewpoint Dependency:** Ensuring that holographic content remains coherent from different viewpoints is a complex problem, especially for dynamic scenes.

- **Content Creation:** Creating holographic content often involves specialized tools and techniques, including the generation of interference patterns and light field data.

- **Integration with Hardware:** Holographic displays may require integration with specific hardware components, such as spatial light modulators or eye-tracking systems.

Holographic displays are at the cutting edge of visual technology, and their potential for transforming how we interact with digital content is immense. As hardware and software technologies continue to advance, the accessibility and capabilities of holographic displays are expected to expand, opening up new possibilities for immersive 3D experiences.

In the subsequent sections of this chapter, we will explore additional topics in volumetric and holographic rendering, including advanced shader techniques, interactive volumetric data visualization, and the challenges of real-time rendering on holographic displays.

Section 6.4: Holographic Shader Techniques

Holographic displays rely on sophisticated shader techniques to create realistic three-dimensional visual experiences. These shaders simulate the complex behavior of light, including diffraction, interference, and refraction, which are fundamental to the illusion of holography. In this section, we will explore the key shader techniques used in holographic rendering.

Simulating Holographic Interference Patterns

Holographic interference patterns are at the heart of holography. These patterns are created by the interference of two coherent light sources, typically a reference beam and an object beam. In holographic shaders, simulating interference patterns involves carefully controlling the phase and intensity of light. This can be achieved through specialized shaders, often written in GLSL (OpenGL Shading Language) or HLSL (High-Level Shading Language).

// Example GLSL shader for simulating holographic interference patterns

void main() {

// Calculate holographic interference effects

// ...

// Output final pixel color

gl_FragColor = finalColor;

}

Refraction and Dispersion

Holographic shaders may also simulate refraction and dispersion, which occur when light passes through transparent or semi-transparent materials. These effects are crucial for creating the illusion of depth and volume in holographic content.

```
// Example GLSL shader for simulating refraction

void main() {

// Calculate refraction effects

// ...

// Output final pixel color

gl_FragColor = finalColor;

}
```

Diffraction Gratings

Diffraction gratings are structures that disperse light into its component colors, creating spectral effects. In holographic shaders, diffraction gratings can be simulated to produce colorful and visually captivating holographic content.

```
// Example GLSL shader for simulating diffraction gratings

void main() {

// Calculate diffraction grating effects

// ...

// Output final pixel color

gl_FragColor = finalColor;

}
```

Holographic Lens Effects

Holographic lenses, often integrated into holographic displays, can be simulated using shaders. These lenses may introduce distortions, aberrations, or other optical effects that need to be accounted for to maintain visual fidelity.

```glsl
// Example GLSL shader for simulating holographic lens effects

void main() {

// Calculate lens effects

// ...

// Output final pixel color

gl_FragColor = finalColor;

}
```

Challenges in Holographic Shader Development

Developing shaders for holographic rendering presents several challenges:

- **Complexity:** Simulating the intricate behavior of light accurately can be highly complex and mathematically demanding.

- **Performance:** Achieving real-time performance while rendering holographic content with advanced shader effects requires optimization.

- **Integration:** Integrating holographic shaders with the overall rendering pipeline, including stereoscopic rendering and real-time interactivity, can be challenging.

- **Content Creation:** Creating holographic shaders often involves specialized tools and expertise in optics and photonics.

Holographic shader development is an evolving field, with ongoing research and innovation aimed at pushing the boundaries of what is possible in holographic displays. As hardware capabilities continue to improve, the potential for more immersive and realistic holographic experiences becomes increasingly achievable.

In the subsequent sections of this chapter, we will continue exploring topics related to volumetric and holographic rendering, including interactive volumetric data visualization and the challenges of real-time rendering on holographic displays.

Section 6.5: Interactive Volumetric Data Visualization

Interactive volumetric data visualization plays a pivotal role in various domains, from medical imaging to scientific simulations and entertainment. This section explores the techniques and considerations for creating interactive volumetric visualizations, leveraging the capabilities of holographic displays and advanced graphics technologies.

Volumetric Data Representation

To create interactive volumetric visualizations, you first need to represent volumetric data effectively. This data can originate from sources like 3D medical scans, scientific simulations, or 3D modeling. Common representations include voxel grids, point clouds, or level sets.

Volume Rendering

Volume rendering is a powerful technique for visualizing volumetric data. It involves simulating the interaction of light with the volume, considering factors like absorption, scattering, and emission. OpenGL provides shaders and techniques for volume rendering, enabling you to visualize complex datasets in real-time.

```glsl
// Example GLSL shader for volume rendering

void main() {

// Perform volume rendering calculations

// ...

// Output final pixel color

gl_FragColor = finalColor;

}
```

Interactive Navigation

Interactive navigation is crucial for exploring volumetric data. On holographic displays, this often involves techniques like hand gestures, voice commands, or gaze-based interactions. Implementing intuitive and responsive navigation is essential for a seamless user experience.

Occlusion and Transparency

Volumetric data can be occluded by other structures within the volume. Properly handling occlusion and transparency is essential for maintaining the visual integrity of the data. Techniques like ray casting and depth peeling can be employed to address these challenges.

Real-time Interaction

Interactive volumetric visualizations demand real-time performance. Optimizing rendering pipelines, leveraging GPU acceleration, and employing level-of-detail techniques are strategies to ensure smooth interactivity, especially on holographic displays with high-resolution requirements.

```cpp
// Example C++ code for real-time interaction with volumetric data

void UpdateVisualization() {

// Handle user interactions

// ...

// Update the rendering based on user input

// ...

}
```

Holographic Considerations

When creating interactive volumetric visualizations for holographic displays, several additional considerations come into play:

- **Stereoscopy:** Ensuring that the visualization provides a 3D perception for both eyes is essential for holographic displays.

- **Holographic Lens Correction:** Correcting for distortions introduced by holographic lenses is crucial to maintain visual accuracy.

- **Light Field Rendering:** Some holographic displays, like light field displays, require rendering from multiple viewpoints to create parallax effects.

- **Gesture and Voice Interaction:** Implementing natural and intuitive interaction methods, such as gesture recognition and voice commands, enhances the user experience.

Interactive volumetric data visualization is a rapidly evolving field with applications in medicine, scientific research, education, and entertainment. As hardware capabilities advance, the potential for creating highly immersive and informative volumetric experiences on holographic displays continues to expand.

Chapter 7: Advanced Real-time Ray Tracing

Section 7.1: Implementing Path Tracing

Path tracing is a rendering technique that simulates the behavior of light rays as they interact with surfaces in a scene. Unlike traditional rasterization-based rendering, path tracing is capable of producing highly realistic global illumination effects, including soft shadows, caustics, and accurate reflections. In this section, we will delve into the principles of path tracing and explore how to implement it using OpenGL or similar graphics APIs.

Understanding Path Tracing

At its core, path tracing is a Monte Carlo method that simulates the path of light rays in reverse. It begins by tracing rays from the camera into the scene, bouncing them off surfaces, and accumulating radiance values at each intersection point. This process continues recursively until a termination condition is met, such as reaching a maximum recursion depth or when a ray escapes the scene.

Key Concepts in Path Tracing:

1. **Ray Generation:** Path tracing starts with the generation of primary rays from the camera's viewpoint. These rays are cast into the scene to collect information about the light arriving at the camera.
2. **Ray Intersection:** When a ray intersects a surface in the scene, the renderer calculates how the surface interacts with the ray. This includes computing surface properties like reflection, refraction, and absorption.

3. **Recursive Rays:** Path tracing often involves recursively tracing secondary rays, such as reflection and refraction rays, to simulate the complex interactions of light.
4. **Light Transport:** Radiance values are accumulated along the path of each ray, taking into account the properties of the surfaces encountered. This includes diffuse reflection, specular reflection, and transmission through transparent materials.

Implementing Path Tracing in OpenGL

Implementing path tracing in OpenGL or similar graphics APIs involves writing shaders that perform ray tracing calculations. These shaders are executed for each pixel in the image, and they trace rays into the scene, accumulating radiance values.

// Example GLSL shader for path tracing

vec3 PathTrace(vec3 rayOrigin, vec3 rayDirection, int depth) {

// Check for termination condition (e.g., maximum depth)

if (depth >= MAX_DEPTH) {

return vec3(0.0);

}

// Perform ray-surface intersection to find the closest surface point

// ...

// Calculate the reflected and refracted rays based on surface properties

// ...

// Recursively trace reflected and refracted rays

```
vec3    reflectedRadiance    =    PathTrace(reflectedRayOrigin,
reflectedRayDirection, depth + 1);

vec3    refractedRadiance    =    PathTrace(refractedRayOrigin,
refractedRayDirection, depth + 1);

// Accumulate radiance values and return the result

vec3    finalRadiance    =    surfaceColor    +    (reflectivity    *
reflectedRadiance) + (transparency * refractedRadiance);

return finalRadiance;

}
```

Challenges and Considerations

Implementing path tracing comes with several challenges:

- **Performance:** Path tracing is computationally intensive and typically slower than rasterization-based rendering. Optimizations, such as importance sampling and denoising, are essential for real-time performance.

- **Complex Scenes:** Handling complex scenes with many surfaces and light sources can be challenging. Techniques like acceleration structures (e.g., BVH) are used to improve ray-triangle intersection performance.

- **Memory Usage:** Path tracing may require significant memory for storing intermediate data, especially in the case of recursive rays.

- **Denoising:** Path tracing often produces noisy images, which need to be denoised using post-processing techniques.

Despite these challenges, path tracing is widely used in the creation of photorealistic computer-generated imagery (CGI) and is an essential technique for achieving realism in rendering. Advances in hardware, such as ray tracing-capable GPUs, have made real-time path tracing increasingly feasible in interactive applications and games.

Section 7.2: Photon Mapping

Photon mapping is a sophisticated global illumination technique used in computer graphics to simulate the complex behavior of light in a scene. Unlike traditional ray tracing or rasterization, photon mapping focuses on capturing indirect illumination effects, including caustics, diffused inter-reflections, and color bleeding. In this section, we will delve into the principles of photon mapping and explore how it can be implemented to enhance the realism of rendered scenes.

Understanding Photon Mapping

Photon mapping operates in two main phases: photon emission and photon gathering.

Photon Emission:

1. **Photon Emission:** During this phase, photons are emitted from light sources into the scene. These photons follow the laws of geometric optics, meaning they travel in straight lines until they encounter a surface.
2. **Photon Interaction:** When a photon strikes a surface, it interacts with the material properties of that surface. Depending on the material, the photon may be absorbed, reflected, or refracted.

3. **Photon Tracing:** Photons that are reflected or refracted continue their path, potentially striking other surfaces and undergoing further interactions.

Photon Gathering:

1. **Photon Gathering:** In the gathering phase, the renderer collects photons that have contributed to the indirect illumination at each point in the scene. This phase involves searching for nearby photons and estimating the indirect lighting effect they contribute.
2. **Radiance Estimation:** To estimate the radiance at a point in the scene, the renderer performs a weighted sum of photon contributions. This involves considering the distance and direction between the photons and the point of interest.
3. **Caustics and Color Bleeding:** Photon mapping excels at simulating caustics, which are concentrated beams of light formed by reflective or refractive surfaces, and color bleeding, where the color of one surface is influenced by nearby surfaces.

Implementing Photon Mapping

Implementing photon mapping requires several key components, including photon emission, photon tracing, photon storage, and radiance estimation.

```cpp
// Example C++ code for photon mapping

void EmitPhotons(const Scene& scene, PhotonMap& photonMap)
{
    // Emit photons from light sources into the scene
```

```
// ...

// Trace photons through the scene, considering surface interactions

// ...

}

void GatherPhotons(const Scene& scene, PhotonMap& photonMap, Image& renderedImage) {

// For each pixel in the image, gather photons and estimate radiance

// ...

// Apply gathered radiance to the pixel in the rendered image

// ...

}
```

Challenges and Considerations

Photon mapping introduces challenges such as:

- **Photon Distribution:** Achieving a well-distributed set of photons in the scene is crucial for accurate results. Strategies like photon scattering and Russian roulette are used to address this.

- **Photon Storage:** Storing and efficiently accessing a large number of photons can be memory-intensive. Techniques like KD-trees or balanced binary trees are employed for efficient photon storage and retrieval.

- **Performance:** Photon mapping can be computationally expensive. Real-time applications often use photon mapping in combination with other techniques and optimizations to maintain interactive frame rates.

Despite these challenges, photon mapping is a powerful tool for achieving realistic global illumination in computer graphics. It is commonly used in rendering engines for applications ranging from architectural visualization to animated films, adding a high level of visual fidelity to the rendered scenes.

Section 7.3: Radiance and Irradiance Caching

Radiance and irradiance caching is a technique used in computer graphics to accelerate global illumination calculations, particularly for complex scenes. It is based on the concept of caching precomputed radiance or irradiance values at specific points in the scene and reusing them during rendering. This section explores the principles behind radiance and irradiance caching and how they can improve the efficiency and realism of global illumination rendering.

Understanding Radiance and Irradiance

Radiance is the amount of light that flows through a small area in a particular direction. It is a fundamental concept in rendering, representing the flow of light rays in a scene. Radiance is typically expressed as a function of position and direction.

Irradiance is a related concept that measures the incoming light energy per unit area at a specific point on a surface. It represents the illumination received by a surface from all directions. Irradiance is often used to calculate the brightness and color of surfaces in a scene.

Radiance Caching

Radiance caching involves precomputing radiance values at selected points in the scene and storing them in a cache. During rendering, when a ray intersects a cached point, the cached radiance value is used instead of performing additional expensive calculations. This significantly reduces the computational cost of global illumination.

```cpp
// Example C++ code for radiance caching

void ComputeRadianceCache(const Scene& scene, RadianceCache& radianceCache) {

// Precompute radiance values at cache points in the scene

// ...

// Store radiance values in the cache

// ...

}

Radiance LookupRadianceCache(const RadianceCache& radianceCache, const Ray& ray) {

// Check if the ray intersects a cached point

// If yes, return the cached radiance value

// Otherwise, compute radiance as usual

// ...

}
```

Irradiance Caching

Irradiance caching is similar to radiance caching but focuses on precomputing and caching irradiance values at selected points. During rendering, when shading a surface point, the cached irradiance values from nearby cache points are used to calculate the illumination, reducing the need for costly indirect lighting calculations.

```cpp
// Example C++ code for irradiance caching

void        ComputeIrradianceCache(const        Scene&        scene,
IrradianceCache& irradianceCache) {

// Precompute irradiance values at cache points on surfaces

// ...

// Store irradiance values in the cache

// ...

}

Irradiance        LookupIrradianceCache(const        IrradianceCache&
irradianceCache, const SurfacePoint& point) {

// Check if the point is close to a cached location

// If yes, return the cached irradiance value

// Otherwise, compute irradiance as usual

// ...

}
```

Challenges and Considerations

Radiance and irradiance caching can significantly speed up global illumination calculations, but they come with challenges:

- **Cache Quality:** The quality of cached radiance or irradiance values depends on the number and distribution of cache points. Poorly chosen cache points can lead to artifacts.

- **Cache Updates:** The cache needs to be updated dynamically as the scene or lighting changes, which can be complex to implement efficiently.

- **Memory Usage:** Storing and managing cached values can consume a significant amount of memory, especially for large scenes.

Despite these challenges, radiance and irradiance caching are valuable techniques for achieving realistic lighting in complex scenes with global illumination, making them common features in modern rendering engines.

Section 7.4: Real-time Caustics

Real-time caustics are a visually striking phenomenon that occur when light rays are focused or concentrated by reflective or refractive surfaces. Examples of caustics can be seen in the patterns of light at the bottom of a swimming pool or the dappled sunlight patterns under a tree. Achieving real-time caustics in computer graphics is a challenging task due to the complex nature of light transport, but it can greatly enhance the visual realism of a scene. In this section, we will explore techniques for simulating real-time caustics in computer graphics.

Principles of Caustics

Caustics are a result of the concentration of light energy due to the geometry and materials in a scene. There are two main types of caustics:

1. **Refractive Caustics:** These occur when light rays pass through transparent or translucent materials, such as glass or water. The bending of light rays and their concentration at certain points or patterns create refractive caustics.
2. **Reflective Caustics:** Reflective caustics occur when light reflects off surfaces and concentrates at certain points. These are commonly seen with metallic or highly reflective surfaces.

Techniques for Real-time Caustics

Achieving real-time caustics typically involves a combination of techniques, including photon mapping, ray tracing, and shader-based rendering. Here's a high-level overview of the process:

Photon Mapping:

Photon mapping is used to precompute the paths of photons as they interact with surfaces in the scene. This technique allows the renderer to simulate the behavior of light rays and calculate how they concentrate to form caustic patterns.

Photon Tracing:

During rendering, photons are traced from light sources, and their paths are followed as they interact with surfaces. This tracing process is used to identify areas where photons concentrate to form caustics.

Shader-based Rendering:

Shader programs are employed to simulate the concentration of photons at the caustic points. These shaders calculate the final color and intensity of light at each point, creating the caustic effect.

Implementing Real-time Caustics

```cpp
// Example C++ code for real-time caustics

void ComputePhotonPaths(const Scene& scene, PhotonMap& photonMap) {

// Precompute photon paths for caustics

// ...

// Store photon paths in the photon map

// ...

}

void TracePhotons(const Scene& scene, PhotonMap& photonMap)
{

// Trace photons from light sources, considering surface interactions

// ...

// Identify areas of caustic concentration

// ...

}

void RenderCaustics(const Scene& scene, PhotonMap& photonMap, Image& renderedImage) {
```

// Apply shader-based rendering to create caustic effects

// ...

// Combine the caustics with the rest of the scene

// ...

}

Challenges and Considerations

Real-time caustics present several challenges:

- **Performance:** Calculating caustics in real-time can be computationally expensive, especially for scenes with many reflective or refractive surfaces.

- **Memory Usage:** Storing photon maps and related data structures can consume a significant amount of memory.

- **Complex Scene Interaction:** Handling complex scene geometries and materials that affect caustic patterns can be challenging.

Despite these challenges, real-time caustics are a powerful tool for enhancing the visual quality of computer-generated scenes, especially for applications like architectural visualization, games, and simulations where realism is essential.

Section 7.5: Noise Reduction Techniques

Noise reduction is a critical aspect of real-time ray tracing and global illumination rendering. Noise in rendered images can be distracting and reduce the overall quality of the visual output. In this section, we will explore various techniques and strategies used to reduce noise in real-time ray-traced images.

Understanding Noise in Ray Tracing

Noise in ray-traced images appears as random variations in pixel values, often characterized by speckles or grainy patterns. It is primarily caused by the stochastic nature of sampling rays and the limited number of samples used to approximate complex lighting and reflection interactions.

Techniques for Noise Reduction

1. Increasing Sample Count:

One of the most straightforward ways to reduce noise is to increase the number of rays or samples used in the rendering process. This can lead to smoother and less noisy images but comes at the cost of increased computational requirements.

2. Denoising Filters:

Denoising filters are post-processing techniques applied to the rendered image. They analyze the image and attempt to remove noise while preserving important details. Common denoising filters include bilateral filters, median filters, and neural network-based approaches.

```cpp
// Example C++ code for applying a denoising filter

Image DenoiseImage(const Image& noisyImage) {

// Apply a denoising filter to the noisy image
```

```cpp
Image denoisedImage;

// ...

return denoisedImage;

}
```

3. Variance-based Sampling:

Variance-based sampling techniques adaptively allocate more samples to noisy or challenging areas of the scene, effectively reducing noise where it is most noticeable.

4. Importance Sampling:

Importance sampling focuses on sampling rays more frequently in directions that contribute the most to the final image. By allocating more samples to critical areas, noise can be reduced more efficiently.

5. Temporal Accumulation:

In real-time applications like games, temporal accumulation involves averaging the results of multiple frames. This approach leverages the coherence between consecutive frames to reduce noise.

```cpp
// Example C++ code for temporal accumulation

Image AccumulateFrames(const Image& currentFrame, const Image& previousAccumulation, int frameCount) {

// Combine the current frame with previous accumulations

Image accumulatedImage;
```

```
// ...

return accumulatedImage;

}
```

Hybrid Approaches

Many real-time ray tracing systems employ a combination of these techniques to strike a balance between rendering speed and noise reduction. For instance, importance sampling may be used to allocate samples smartly, while denoising filters can further clean up the image.

Challenges and Considerations

- **Performance Trade-offs:** Increasing sample counts or applying complex denoising filters can impact real-time performance, making it necessary to find the right trade-off between noise reduction and frame rate.

- **Artifacts:** Aggressive noise reduction techniques may inadvertently introduce artifacts or blur important details in the image.

- **Scene Complexity:** Noise reduction becomes more challenging in scenes with complex lighting, materials, and reflections.

Noise reduction is an ongoing area of research in real-time ray tracing, and developers are continually exploring innovative approaches to achieve high-quality, noise-free images in interactive applications.

Chapter 8: Realistic Atmospheric and Weather Effects

Section 8.1: Atmospheric Scattering

Realistic rendering of atmospheric effects plays a crucial role in creating immersive and visually stunning virtual environments. Atmospheric scattering simulates the interaction of sunlight with the Earth's atmosphere, leading to various optical phenomena like the blue sky, sunsets, and the scattering of light. In this section, we will explore the fundamentals of atmospheric scattering and how it contributes to the realism of computer-generated scenes.

Basics of Atmospheric Scattering

Atmospheric scattering is the process by which sunlight interacts with tiny particles and gas molecules in the Earth's atmosphere. This interaction results in the scattering of light in different directions, affecting the color and appearance of the sky. Several key principles govern atmospheric scattering:

1. **Rayleigh Scattering:** This is the dominant form of scattering at shorter wavelengths, such as blue and violet light. It is responsible for the blue color of the daytime sky.
2. **Mie Scattering:** Mie scattering occurs when particles are larger than the wavelength of light and is responsible for scattering at longer wavelengths, creating effects like haze and cloud scattering.

Simulating Atmospheric Scattering

Simulating realistic atmospheric scattering in computer graphics involves complex calculations to approximate the behavior of light as it traverses the atmosphere. The key steps in simulating atmospheric scattering include:

1. Ray Tracing:

Rays of light are traced through the atmosphere to simulate their interaction with air molecules and particles.

2. Scattering Equations:

Equations, such as the Rayleigh and Mie scattering equations, are used to model the scattering of light at different wavelengths and directions.

3. Sky Color Calculation:

The scattering equations are applied to calculate the color of the sky based on the angle of the incoming and outgoing light rays.

4. Realistic Sky Domains:

Techniques are employed to create realistic sky gradients, taking into account the observer's position on the Earth's surface.

Implementing Atmospheric Scattering

```cpp
// Example C++ code for simulating atmospheric scattering

Color CalculateSkyColor(Vector3 viewDirection, Vector3 sunDirection) {

// Implement the Rayleigh and Mie scattering equations

// to calculate the sky color based on view and sun direction.
```

```
Color skyColor;

// ...

return skyColor;

}

void RenderScene() {

// Render the scene, incorporating atmospheric scattering effects.

// ...

}
```

Applications of Atmospheric Scattering

Realistic atmospheric scattering is essential in various applications, including video games, flight simulators, and architectural visualization. It enhances the visual quality of scenes by adding depth, realism, and a sense of atmosphere.

Challenges and Optimization

Implementing atmospheric scattering in real-time applications can be computationally intensive. Optimization techniques, such as precomputing scattering tables and using approximations, are often used to achieve a balance between realism and performance.

In summary, atmospheric scattering is a fundamental component of rendering realistic outdoor environments in computer graphics. Understanding and simulating the behavior of light in the atmosphere is crucial for creating immersive and visually appealing virtual worlds.

Section 8.2: Real-time Cloud Simulation

Realistic cloud simulation is a key element in creating immersive outdoor environments in computer graphics. Clouds not only contribute to the visual beauty of a scene but also play a significant role in lighting, shadowing, and weather effects. In this section, we will delve into real-time cloud simulation techniques and how they are implemented to enhance the visual quality of 3D environments.

Importance of Cloud Simulation

Clouds are dynamic and ever-changing, and they have a substantial impact on the appearance of outdoor scenes. Their presence can significantly influence the lighting conditions, creating variations in shadows, reflections, and the overall atmosphere. Accurate cloud simulation adds depth and realism to virtual worlds, making them more engaging for viewers.

Cloud Modeling Techniques

1. Volumetric Clouds:

Volumetric cloud models represent clouds as three-dimensional volumes within the scene. These volumes are rendered as participating media, allowing light to interact with cloud particles inside the volume. Techniques like ray marching and scattering equations are used to simulate the behavior of light within the cloud.

2. Texture-based Clouds:

Texture-based cloud models use 2D or 3D textures to represent the appearance of clouds. These textures are applied to flat or semi-transparent planes within the scene. Techniques like shader-based blending are used to achieve realistic cloud formations and animations.

3. Particle Systems:

Clouds can also be simulated using particle systems, where individual cloud particles are represented and controlled in the 3D environment. These particles interact with light and each other to create cloud-like formations.

Implementing Real-time Clouds

// Example C++ code for rendering volumetric clouds

void RenderVolumetricClouds(Camera camera, CloudVolume cloudVolume) {

// Perform ray marching through the cloud volume to render clouds.

// Calculate lighting interactions and shadowing.

// ...

}

// Example C++ code for rendering texture-based clouds

void RenderTextureBasedClouds(Camera camera, CloudTexture cloudTexture) {

// Render flat cloud planes using texture-based techniques.

// Apply shaders for blending and animation.

// ...

}

```cpp
// Example C++ code for simulating cloud particles

void SimulateCloudParticles(float deltaTime) {

// Update the positions and behaviors of individual cloud particles.

// Handle interactions with light and other particles.

// ...

}
```

Dynamic Cloud Animation

Real-time cloud simulation often includes dynamic cloud animation to mimic the movement and evolution of real clouds. Techniques such as noise functions and wind simulations are used to create realistic cloud motion over time.

Challenges and Optimization

Implementing real-time cloud simulation can be computationally intensive, especially when dealing with volumetric clouds and complex lighting interactions. Optimization techniques, such as level-of-detail (LOD) rendering and caching, are commonly employed to maintain performance while achieving realistic results.

In conclusion, real-time cloud simulation is a crucial component of rendering outdoor environments in computer graphics. By accurately modeling the behavior of clouds and their interaction with light, developers can create visually stunning and immersive virtual worlds.

Section 8.3: Dynamic Weather Systems

Dynamic weather systems are an essential feature in modern computer graphics to create immersive outdoor scenes that respond to changing weather conditions. These systems simulate various atmospheric phenomena such as rain, snow, fog, and even storms, enhancing the realism and interactivity of virtual environments. In this section, we will explore the significance of dynamic weather systems and their implementation in real-time graphics.

Importance of Dynamic Weather

Dynamic weather systems contribute significantly to the visual and atmospheric richness of a virtual world. They enable a more engaging and interactive experience for users by introducing variability and unpredictability to the environment. Here are some key aspects of dynamic weather:

- **Variation:** Weather systems introduce variation in lighting, visibility, and environmental conditions, making scenes feel more dynamic and less repetitive.

- **Aesthetics:** Weather effects such as rain, snow, and fog can enhance the visual beauty of a scene, adding depth and realism.

- **Gameplay:** Weather can impact gameplay by affecting character movement, visibility, and strategy. For example, rain can make surfaces slippery, affecting control.

Simulating Dynamic Weather

Implementing dynamic weather systems involves a combination of artistic and technical approaches:

1. Weather Patterns:

Developers design weather patterns that define how various weather conditions change over time. This includes defining the likelihood and intensity of rain, snow, fog, or storms.

2. Particle Systems:

Weather effects like rain and snow are often realized using particle systems. Particles are emitted into the scene, and their behavior is controlled to simulate precipitation. For example, raindrops may fall and interact with the environment.

3. Lighting and Shading:

Dynamic weather requires adjustments to lighting and shading. For instance, during a storm, the sky becomes darker, and lightning may briefly illuminate the scene. These changes affect the overall appearance of objects and characters.

Implementing Dynamic Weather

```cpp
// Example C++ code for dynamic weather simulation

void SimulateDynamicWeather(float deltaTime, WeatherPattern currentWeather) {

// Update weather conditions based on predefined patterns.

// Adjust particle systems for rain, snow, or fog.

// Modify lighting and shading parameters.

//...
```

```
}

void RenderScene(Camera camera) {

// Render the scene with dynamic weather effects.

// Apply changes in lighting, particle systems, and shaders.

// ...

}
```

Dynamic Weather Interactions

Dynamic weather systems can interact with other aspects of the virtual environment. For example, rain can create puddles, and snow can accumulate on surfaces. Characters and vehicles may respond to weather conditions, impacting their behavior and appearance.

Challenges and Optimization

Implementing dynamic weather systems in real-time graphics can be computationally expensive, especially when dealing with complex particle simulations and dynamic lighting changes. Developers often employ optimization techniques such as level-of-detail (LOD) for weather effects and caching to maintain smooth performance.

In summary, dynamic weather systems are a vital element in creating realistic and immersive outdoor environments in computer graphics. They add variability and unpredictability to virtual worlds, making them more visually engaging and interactive.

Section 8.4: Natural Phenomena (e.g., Rainbows, Aurora)

In the realm of computer graphics, the depiction of natural phenomena can elevate the visual richness of a virtual world. Natural phenomena, such as rainbows and auroras, are captivating and add a layer of beauty and realism to outdoor scenes. In this section, we'll explore the significance of representing these natural wonders in real-time graphics and how they are implemented.

The Beauty of Natural Phenomena

1. Rainbows:

Rainbows are optical and meteorological phenomena that occur when sunlight is refracted, or bent, as it passes through water droplets in the atmosphere. This bending of light causes the sunlight to separate into its constituent colors, creating the iconic arc of colors that we associate with rainbows. The appearance of a rainbow is influenced by factors like the size of water droplets and the angle of sunlight.

2. Auroras:

Auroras, also known as the Northern and Southern Lights (Aurora Borealis and Aurora Australis), are natural light displays in the Earth's sky. They are caused by charged particles from the sun colliding with gas molecules in the Earth's atmosphere. Auroras often appear as colorful curtains or waves of light in polar regions.

Simulating Natural Phenomena

The simulation of natural phenomena in computer graphics involves the following key elements:

1. Physics Simulation:

To simulate rainbows, the physics of light refraction through water droplets must be accurately modeled. Similarly, simulating auroras requires an understanding of the interaction between charged particles and the Earth's magnetic field.

2. Particle Systems:

In many cases, particle systems are used to simulate the behavior of elements in natural phenomena. For instance, raindrop particles are employed to create the appearance of rain in a scene. These particles interact with light to produce the effect of rainbows.

3. Lighting and Shading:

Proper lighting and shading techniques are crucial for representing natural phenomena realistically. For rainbows, the dispersion of light into colors and the bending of light within water droplets must be accurately portrayed. For auroras, the interaction of charged particles with the atmosphere results in the emission of light, which must be rendered realistically.

Implementing Natural Phenomena

// Example C++ code for simulating rainbows

```
void    SimulateRainbows(Camera    camera,    RaindropParticles
raindrops) {

// Calculate the refraction and dispersion of light through raindrops.

// Render the rainbow effect based on physics simulations.

// ...

}

// Example C++ code for simulating auroras

void    SimulateAuroras(Camera    camera,    AuroraParticles
chargedParticles) {

// Model the interaction of charged particles with the atmosphere.

// Render the colorful light emissions characteristic of auroras.

// ...

}
```

Realism and Artistic Interpretation

While realism is essential in depicting natural phenomena, artistic
interpretation also plays a role. Graphics artists and designers may
adjust parameters and aesthetics to achieve the desired visual impact
and atmosphere in a virtual environment.

Challenges and Optimization

Simulating natural phenomena can be computationally intensive,
particularly when aiming for high levels of realism. Developers often
employ optimization techniques such as particle culling and LOD
rendering to balance visual quality with performance.

In conclusion, the representation of natural phenomena in computer graphics enhances the visual appeal and authenticity of virtual worlds. Whether it's the magical appearance of rainbows or the awe-inspiring display of auroras, these phenomena contribute to the beauty and wonder of the digital realm.

Section 8.5: Earth and Space Rendering Techniques

Earth and space rendering techniques are essential components of computer graphics, particularly for creating expansive and realistic environments in games, simulations, and visualizations. In this section, we'll delve into the significance of rendering Earth and space scenes and explore the various techniques used to achieve stunning visual results.

Realism and Scale

1. Earth Rendering:

Rendering the Earth's surface requires attention to detail, from the textures of land and water to the depiction of atmospheric effects like clouds and haze. Achieving realism involves using high-resolution texture maps and advanced shading models to simulate the way light interacts with the Earth's surface.

2. Space Rendering:

Space scenes often encompass vast distances, requiring accurate representation of celestial bodies like stars, planets, and galaxies. The scale of space rendering is staggering, and achieving realistic proportions and lighting conditions is crucial for an immersive experience.

Earth Rendering Techniques

1. Terrain Generation:

Generating realistic terrains involves algorithms like fractal-based techniques, procedural generation, and heightmap rendering. These methods create diverse landscapes, from mountains to valleys, with detailed texture mapping.

2. Atmospheric Scattering:

Earth's atmosphere plays a significant role in its appearance. Atmospheric scattering models simulate the scattering of light by air molecules and particles, affecting the color of the sky, the appearance of sunsets, and the visibility of distant objects.

3. Dynamic Weather Systems:

As discussed in previous sections, dynamic weather systems contribute to Earth rendering by introducing weather effects such as rain, snow, and fog. These effects create variability and enhance realism.

Space Rendering Techniques

1. Star and Galaxy Rendering:

Stars and galaxies are often represented using point sprites or volumetric techniques. Realistic rendering involves modeling the distribution of stars in the night sky and simulating the appearance of galaxies and nebulae.

2. Planetary Rendering:

Planets and celestial bodies are rendered with high-resolution textures and shaders to depict surface features, atmospheres, and dynamic lighting conditions. Rendering realistic planets involves attention to detail and accurate modeling of atmospheric effects.

Implementing Earth and Space Rendering

// Example C++ code for Earth rendering

void RenderEarthScene(Camera camera, EarthSurface surface, Atmosphere atmosphere) {

// Render the Earth's surface with detailed terrain, water, and texture mapping.

// Apply atmospheric scattering to simulate Earth's atmosphere.

// Handle dynamic weather effects.

// ...

}

// Example C++ code for space rendering

void RenderSpaceScene(Camera camera, CelestialBodies stars, Planets planets) {

// Render stars, galaxies, and other celestial objects.

// Simulate the appearance and movement of planets.

```
// Handle dynamic lighting and shadows in space scenes.

// ...

}
```

Challenges and Optimization

Rendering Earth and space scenes can be computationally demanding due to the large scale and complexity of these environments. Optimizations often include level-of-detail (LOD) techniques, culling, and the use of precomputed data to achieve a balance between visual quality and performance.

In conclusion, Earth and space rendering techniques are crucial for creating visually stunning and immersive environments in computer graphics. Whether it's capturing the beauty of our planet or venturing into the vastness of space, these techniques enable us to explore and experience the wonders of the natural world and beyond within the digital realm.

Chapter 9: Hardware and Driver Deep Dive

Section 9.1: Understanding Graphics Hardware Architecture

Understanding the architecture of graphics hardware is fundamental for graphics programmers and developers. It forms the basis for optimizing graphics applications, achieving better performance, and leveraging hardware-specific features. In this section, we will explore the core concepts of graphics hardware architecture and its relevance in the field of computer graphics.

Graphics Processing Unit (GPU)

At the heart of graphics hardware is the Graphics Processing Unit (GPU). The GPU is designed specifically for rendering graphics and performs the complex calculations required for rendering scenes, applying shaders, and managing textures and geometry. Modern GPUs are highly parallel processors, capable of handling thousands of tasks simultaneously.

Pipeline Architecture

Graphics rendering is a highly structured process that occurs in stages. The GPU pipeline is a series of stages through which data flows, undergoing transformations at each stage. The primary stages of a typical GPU pipeline include:

1. Vertex Processing:

In this stage, vertices and their attributes are transformed from object space to screen space. Vertex shaders are used to perform operations on individual vertices.

2. Geometry Processing:

Geometry shaders operate on groups of vertices, creating new vertices or modifying existing ones. This stage is responsible for tessellation and generating additional geometry.

3. Rasterization:

Rasterization converts geometric primitives (e.g., triangles) into fragments or pixels. It determines which fragments are visible and passes them to the next stage.

4. Fragment Processing:

Fragment shaders process individual fragments, calculating colors, textures, and other attributes. This stage is where pixel values are computed.

5. Output Merger:

The output merger stage combines the results of fragment processing, handles depth testing, and writes the final pixel values to the framebuffer.

Parallelism and SIMD Execution

Modern GPUs rely heavily on parallelism to achieve high performance. They utilize a Single Instruction, Multiple Data (SIMD) architecture, where multiple data elements are processed simultaneously using a single instruction. This design allows GPUs to process large datasets efficiently.

Memory Hierarchy

Graphics hardware includes a hierarchy of memory types with varying access speeds and sizes. These include registers, local memory, shared memory, and global memory. Efficient memory management is crucial for optimizing performance.

Specialized Units

In addition to the main pipeline, GPUs often feature specialized units for specific tasks. For example, texture units handle texture sampling, and compute units are designed for general-purpose computing (GPGPU). These units enable GPUs to perform a wide range of tasks beyond graphics rendering.

Understanding graphics hardware architecture empowers developers to make informed decisions when designing graphics applications. It enables the utilization of GPU features for enhanced performance and the optimization of algorithms to leverage the parallel processing capabilities of modern GPUs.

Section 9.2: Driver Internals and Optimization

Graphics drivers serve as a critical interface between the operating system, applications, and the graphics hardware. Understanding driver internals is essential for graphics programmers to optimize their applications, ensure compatibility, and leverage the full capabilities of the underlying hardware. In this section, we will delve into the intricacies of graphics drivers and explore optimization techniques.

Driver Components

Graphics drivers consist of several key components, each responsible for specific tasks:

1. Kernel-Mode Driver:

The kernel-mode driver operates at the lowest level and communicates directly with the graphics hardware. It manages hardware resources, memory allocation, and provides an interface for user-mode applications.

2. User-Mode Driver:

The user-mode driver acts as an intermediary between the application and the kernel-mode driver. It translates high-level graphics API calls (e.g., OpenGL, DirectX) into commands that the kernel-mode driver can understand.

3. Control Panel and Configuration:

Graphics drivers often include a control panel that allows users to customize graphics settings. This panel communicates with the user-mode driver to apply these settings.

4. Shader Compiler:

Modern graphics drivers include a shader compiler that translates high-level shader code into bytecode or machine code that the GPU can execute.

Optimization Techniques

Optimizing graphics applications often involves collaboration with graphics driver developers. However, there are several practices that graphics programmers can implement to ensure better compatibility and performance:

1. Use Vendor-Specific Extensions Sparingly:

While vendor-specific extensions can provide access to advanced features, they may limit the portability of your application. It's essential to use them judiciously and provide fallbacks for platforms that do not support these extensions.

2. Minimize Driver Overhead:

Graphics APIs like DirectX 12 and Vulkan offer lower-level access to the GPU, reducing driver overhead. Leveraging these APIs can lead to better performance, especially in CPU-bound scenarios.

3. Profile and Benchmark:

Profiling tools can help identify bottlenecks in your application. By understanding where the performance bottlenecks lie, you can work with driver developers to address these issues.

4. Update Drivers Regularly:

Keeping graphics drivers up to date is essential for compatibility and performance. New driver versions often include bug fixes and optimizations that can benefit your application.

5. Test on Multiple Hardware Configurations:

To ensure compatibility, it's crucial to test your application on a variety of hardware configurations. Different GPUs and driver versions may behave differently.

Shader Compilation and Optimization

Shader compilation is a crucial aspect of graphics programming. While shaders are typically written in high-level languages like HLSL or GLSL, they are compiled into GPU-specific code. To optimize shaders:

1. Reduce Redundancy:

Eliminate redundant calculations and operations in your shaders to reduce computational load.

2. Minimize Register Pressure:

GPUs have a limited number of registers, and exceeding this limit can lead to performance penalties. Optimize your shaders to minimize register usage.

3. *Avoid Dynamic Branching:*

Dynamic branching in shaders can be inefficient, as it can lead to divergence in SIMD execution. Minimize branching and use static branching when possible.

Understanding driver internals and optimization techniques is crucial for graphics programmers aiming to create efficient and compatible applications. Collaboration between graphics programmers and driver developers can lead to better performance and improved user experiences in graphics-intensive applications.

Section 9.3: Hardware Tessellation Techniques

Hardware tessellation is a powerful feature offered by modern GPUs that allows for the dynamic subdivision of geometry, enabling more detailed and smoother surfaces. Tessellation techniques are widely used in computer graphics, especially for terrain rendering, character modeling, and smooth curves. In this section, we will explore hardware tessellation in-depth and understand how it can be leveraged for optimized graphics.

Tessellation Overview

Tessellation involves subdividing a simple geometric shape, such as a triangle, into smaller, more detailed triangles. This process increases the level of detail in a model or surface. Hardware tessellation consists of three key stages:

1. Tessellation Control Shader (TCS):

The TCS is responsible for controlling the tessellation level and determining how the original geometry should be subdivided. It takes control points as input and calculates tessellation factors based on factors like distance from the camera.

2. Tessellation Evaluation Shader (TES):

The TES is responsible for generating the vertices of the subdivided triangles. It takes the control points and tessellation factors from the TCS and calculates the final positions of the vertices.

3. Tessellator:

The tessellator is a fixed-function unit within the GPU that takes the output of the TES and subdivides the triangles accordingly. It generates the additional vertices required for the subdivided triangles.

Benefits of Hardware Tessellation

Hardware tessellation offers several benefits for graphics rendering:

1. Increased Detail:

Tessellation allows for the dynamic increase in the level of detail, which is particularly useful for objects that need to appear more detailed when viewed up close.

2. Smooth Curves:

Tessellation can be used to generate smooth curves and surfaces, improving the overall visual quality of rendered objects.

3. Reduced Memory Usage:

Instead of storing highly detailed models with a large number of vertices, tessellation allows you to store lower-detail models and generate higher-detail geometry as needed. This reduces memory consumption.

Tessellation Techniques

To effectively use hardware tessellation, consider the following techniques:

1. Level of Detail (LOD) Management:

Dynamically adjust the tessellation level based on the distance from the camera. Use higher tessellation levels for close objects and lower levels for distant ones to optimize performance.

2. Displacement Mapping:

Combine tessellation with displacement mapping. Displacement maps contain height information that can be used to create detailed surface geometry, especially for terrain rendering.

3. Culling and LOD Transition:

Implement culling techniques to avoid tessellating geometry that is not visible. Additionally, ensure smooth LOD transitions to avoid noticeable changes in geometry detail.

Tessellation Pitfalls

While tessellation is a powerful tool, it can also introduce performance challenges if not used carefully:

1. Over-Tessellation:

Excessive tessellation can overwhelm the GPU and lead to performance degradation. It's essential to find the right balance between detail and performance.

2. Shader Complexity:

Tessellation shaders can be complex. Ensure that your shaders are optimized and do not introduce bottlenecks in the rendering pipeline.

3. Memory Consumption:

While tessellation can reduce memory usage for models, it can increase memory usage for control points and tessellation factors. Monitor memory consumption carefully.

Hardware tessellation is a valuable feature that can significantly enhance the visual quality of graphics applications. By understanding the principles and techniques of tessellation, graphics programmers can optimize their applications for better performance and stunning visual effects.

Section 9.4: Low-level GPU Programming

Low-level GPU programming involves interacting with the graphics hardware at a level closer to the metal. While modern graphics APIs like DirectX and Vulkan provide higher-level abstractions for graphics rendering, low-level programming offers more control and optimization opportunities. In this section, we will explore the fundamentals of low-level GPU programming and its benefits.

Understanding the Graphics Pipeline

To program the GPU at a low level, it's crucial to have a deep understanding of the graphics pipeline. The graphics pipeline is the sequence of stages through which data flows to render a 3D scene. These stages include vertex processing, tessellation, geometry shading, pixel shading, and more.

Benefits of Low-level GPU Programming

Low-level GPU programming offers several advantages:

1. Performance Optimization:

Low-level programming allows you to fine-tune every aspect of the rendering process, making it possible to achieve the best performance for your specific application.

2. Reduced Overhead:

High-level graphics APIs come with some level of abstraction, which can introduce overhead. Low-level programming minimizes this overhead, resulting in more efficient code execution.

3. Custom Rendering Techniques:

Low-level programming enables you to implement custom rendering techniques that might not be possible or efficient with high-level APIs.

Graphics API Choices

When engaging in low-level GPU programming, you'll typically work with graphics APIs that provide direct access to the GPU hardware. Two prominent choices are:

1. Vulkan:

Vulkan is an open-standard, cross-platform graphics API that provides extensive control over the GPU. It's known for its performance and flexibility but comes with a steeper learning curve.

2. DirectX 12 (or DirectX 11 with feature-level 11.1):

DirectX 12, part of the DirectX family from Microsoft, is another low-level API. It offers a more Windows-centric approach and is commonly used in Windows-based applications.

Basic Concepts in Low-level Programming

Here are some fundamental concepts and tasks involved in low-level GPU programming:

1. Command Buffers:

Command buffers are used to record a sequence of rendering commands that will be executed by the GPU. These commands include drawing, clearing the frame buffer, and more.

2. Memory Management:

Managing GPU memory is crucial in low-level programming. You'll allocate, map, and synchronize memory buffers to transfer data between the CPU and GPU.

3. Synchronization:

Ensuring proper synchronization between CPU and GPU operations is critical to avoid race conditions and data corruption.

Code Example (Vulkan)

```cpp
// Initialize Vulkan

VkInstance instance;

VkApplicationInfo appInfo = {};

appInfo.sType = VK_STRUCTURE_TYPE_APPLICATION_INFO;

appInfo.pApplicationName = "My Vulkan App";
```

```cpp
// ... (other application info)

VkInstanceCreateInfo createInfo = {};

createInfo.sType                                    =
VK_STRUCTURE_TYPE_INSTANCE_CREATE_INFO;

createInfo.pApplicationInfo = &appInfo;

// ... (instance creation)

vkCreateInstance(&createInfo, nullptr, &instance);

// Create a Vulkan device

VkDevice device;

VkDeviceCreateInfo deviceInfo = {};

deviceInfo.sType                                    =
VK_STRUCTURE_TYPE_DEVICE_CREATE_INFO;

// ... (device creation)

vkCreateDevice(physicalDevice, &deviceInfo, nullptr, &device);

// Create a command buffer

VkCommandBuffer commandBuffer;

VkCommandBufferAllocateInfo allocInfo = {};

allocInfo.sType                                     =
VK_STRUCTURE_TYPE_COMMAND_BUFFER_ALLOCATE_IN

allocInfo.level                                     =
VK_COMMAND_BUFFER_LEVEL_PRIMARY;

allocInfo.commandPool = commandPool;
```

```cpp
allocInfo.commandBufferCount = 1;

vkAllocateCommandBuffers(device, &allocInfo, &commandBuffer);

// Record rendering commands

vkBeginCommandBuffer(commandBuffer, &beginInfo);

// ... (rendering commands)

vkEndCommandBuffer(commandBuffer);

// Submit the command buffer for execution

VkSubmitInfo submitInfo = {};

submitInfo.sType = VK_STRUCTURE_TYPE_SUBMIT_INFO;

submitInfo.commandBufferCount = 1;

submitInfo.pCommandBuffers = &commandBuffer;

vkQueueSubmit(graphicsQueue, 1, &submitInfo, VK_NULL_HANDLE);
```

Low-level GPU programming requires a solid understanding of the chosen API and the graphics pipeline. It's a powerful approach for developers who need fine-grained control over graphics rendering and optimization. However, it also demands careful management of resources and synchronization to ensure correct and efficient rendering.

Section 9.5: Future of Graphics Hardware

The future of graphics hardware holds exciting prospects, driven by advancements in technology, evolving user demands, and emerging trends. In this section, we'll explore some of the key directions and innovations expected in the field of graphics hardware.

1. Ray Tracing Acceleration:

Ray tracing has gained significant attention for its ability to produce stunningly realistic visuals. Future graphics hardware is likely to feature dedicated ray tracing hardware, making real-time ray tracing more accessible and efficient. This technology will enable more lifelike reflections, shadows, and lighting effects in games and applications.

2. AI Integration:

Artificial intelligence (AI) is becoming increasingly integrated into graphics hardware. AI can be used for upscaling lower-resolution content, enhancing anti-aliasing techniques, and even generating content procedurally. Future GPUs are expected to have AI-specific cores for tasks like denoising and predictive rendering.

3. Quantum Computing:

While still in its infancy, quantum computing holds promise for graphics-related tasks. Quantum computers could revolutionize simulations, optimization, and rendering algorithms. As quantum hardware matures, it may find applications in areas like molecular modeling and complex physical simulations.

4. Real-time Global Illumination:

Achieving real-time global illumination has been a long-standing challenge in computer graphics. Future hardware may feature dedicated solutions for global illumination calculations, enabling more realistic lighting in games and simulations without compromising performance.

5. Holographic Displays:

Graphics hardware may evolve to support holographic displays, offering immersive 3D experiences without the need for specialized glasses or VR headsets. This technology could find applications in gaming, design, medical visualization, and more.

6. Energy Efficiency:

With a growing focus on sustainability, future graphics hardware is likely to prioritize energy efficiency. Manufacturers will aim to deliver high-performance GPUs with reduced power consumption, benefiting both desktop and mobile devices.

7. Neuromorphic Hardware:

Neuromorphic hardware, inspired by the human brain's neural networks, could play a role in graphics processing. These architectures can excel in pattern recognition and complex data processing, potentially enhancing AI-driven graphics tasks.

8. Optical Computing:

Optical computing, which uses light instead of electrical signals, is a promising area of research. It has the potential to significantly speed up certain graphics computations, such as Fourier transforms and image processing.

9. Unified Memory Architectures:

Future GPUs may adopt unified memory architectures that blur the line between CPU and GPU memory. This would simplify data sharing and reduce the need for complex memory management in software.

10. Customization and Configurability:

Graphics hardware may become more customizable, allowing developers and users to configure the hardware for specific tasks. This flexibility can lead to improved performance and efficiency.

As technology continues to advance, graphics hardware will play a pivotal role in shaping the visual experiences of tomorrow. Developers and researchers in the field of computer graphics will need to stay at the forefront of these innovations to harness their full potential and create even more immersive and realistic digital worlds.

Chapter 10: Immersive Audio Techniques

Section 10.1: Binaural and 3D Audio

In the realm of immersive experiences, audio plays an equally crucial role as visuals. Achieving a high level of realism in audio enhances immersion, whether in virtual reality (VR) environments, video games, or simulations. Binaural and 3D audio techniques are at the forefront of creating spatially accurate soundscapes that can transport users to different places and situations. In this section, we'll delve into the concept of binaural and 3D audio and how they are leveraged for immersive applications.

1. Understanding Binaural Audio:

Binaural audio is a technique that simulates the way humans perceive sound in three dimensions using only two ears. It relies on the principle that the human brain can determine the direction and distance of a sound source based on the subtle differences in the sound as it reaches each ear. Binaural audio recordings use specialized microphones to capture sound in a way that mimics this natural process.

2. Head-Related Transfer Functions (HRTFs):

Central to binaural audio is the concept of Head-Related Transfer Functions (HRTFs). HRTFs are filters that account for the unique shape and characteristics of an individual's ears and head. By convolving audio signals with the appropriate HRTF, it's possible to create a convincing illusion of sound coming from different directions.

3. Creating Realistic Soundscapes:

In applications like VR, binaural audio is used to create realistic soundscapes that correspond to the virtual environment. As the user moves their head, the audio should change dynamically to match their perspective, enhancing the sense of presence.

4. 3D Audio vs. Binaural Audio:

While binaural audio is a subset of 3D audio, the terms are sometimes used interchangeably. 3D audio encompasses a broader range of techniques, including ambisonics and object-based audio, which can create immersive sound experiences not limited to binaural rendering.

5. Hardware and Software Implementations:

Implementing binaural and 3D audio requires both hardware and software components. Specialized headphones or earphones are often used to deliver the binaural audio experience, while software algorithms and audio engines handle the spatial audio processing.

6. Applications:

Binaural and 3D audio find applications in VR and AR experiences, gaming, cinematic VR, architectural simulations, and even therapy. For example, in VR gaming, accurate spatial audio cues are essential for gameplay, as they help players locate enemies or objects based on sound.

7. Challenges and Future Developments:

Challenges in implementing binaural and 3D audio include the need for personalized HRTFs, computational demands, and issues related to latency. Future developments may involve more efficient algorithms, improved hardware, and methods for capturing individualized HRTFs easily.

8. Audio Shaders and Processing:

In the context of gaming and interactive applications, audio shaders and real-time audio processing are used to enhance the spatial audio experience. These shaders can simulate audio reflections, occlusions, and diffractions, making sound interactions with the environment more realistic.

9. Accessibility Considerations:

Immersive audio should also consider accessibility. Providing options for users with hearing impairments is essential. Techniques like audio spatialization can help tailor the audio experience to individual needs.

10. Future Potential:

As hardware and software continue to advance, binaural and 3D audio have the potential to become even more convincing and integral to immersive experiences. Their application extends beyond entertainment to education, therapy, and various industries seeking realistic simulations.

Binaural and 3D audio are transformative technologies that contribute significantly to the overall immersion and realism of virtual environments and interactive experiences. Whether it's the subtle rustling of leaves in a virtual forest or the precise positioning of virtual objects in a game, spatial audio techniques add depth and authenticity to the auditory component of immersive content.

Section 10.2: Real-time Reverberation

Techniques

In the realm of immersive audio, achieving realism goes beyond the precise positioning of sound sources; it also involves accurately simulating the acoustic properties of the virtual environment. One crucial aspect of this simulation is reverberation. Reverberation refers to the persistence of sound in an environment after the sound source has stopped emitting. Think of the way sound lingers and bounces off surfaces in a cathedral or an empty room. Real-time reverberation techniques are essential for making virtual spaces sound convincing.

1. Importance of Reverberation:

Reverberation plays a significant role in how we perceive the size and material of a room, as well as the distance of sound sources within it. Without proper reverberation, audio in virtual environments can sound flat and disconnected from the surroundings.

2. Convolution Reverb:

One common method for achieving realistic reverberation is convolution reverb. This technique involves capturing the impulse response of a real-world space, which represents how that space responds to a short, loud sound (like a clap). By convolving the audio with this impulse response, virtual sounds can inherit the acoustic characteristics of the real space.

3. Real-time Convolution:

Achieving real-time convolution reverb can be computationally demanding. Advanced hardware and software solutions are employed to ensure that the convolution process doesn't introduce noticeable latency. This is crucial for maintaining a seamless audio experience, especially in interactive applications.

4. Parameterization and Control:

Real-time reverberation algorithms often allow for the adjustment of parameters such as reverb time (how long sound lingers), early reflections (the first bounces of sound), and diffusion (how spread out the reflections are). These parameters can be tweaked to match the acoustic characteristics of different virtual environments.

5. Spatialization and Reverberation:

Combining spatial audio techniques (like binaural rendering) with real-time reverberation adds another layer of realism. Sound sources can be spatialized in 3D space, and their interactions with the environment's acoustics can be accurately modeled.

6. Interactive Environments:

In interactive applications like games, real-time reverberation techniques need to adapt to dynamic changes in the virtual environment. For example, if a character moves from a small, reflective room into a large, open courtyard, the reverb characteristics should change accordingly.

7. Hardware Acceleration:

High-quality real-time reverberation often requires dedicated hardware acceleration. Some modern GPUs and DSPs include specialized audio processing units for handling complex acoustic simulations efficiently.

8. Future Trends:

As computational power continues to increase, we can expect even more realistic and interactive real-time reverberation techniques. These advancements will enhance the sense of presence in virtual environments and further blur the line between the real and virtual worlds.

9. Integration Challenges:

Integrating real-time reverberation into existing audio engines and frameworks can be complex. Developers need to consider how audio sources interact with the environment, how sound propagates, and how to maintain optimal performance.

10. Audio Rendering Engines:

Various audio rendering engines and middleware provide solutions for real-time reverberation. These tools often come with a range of presets for different environments and materials, making it easier for developers to achieve convincing audio environments.

In conclusion, real-time reverberation techniques are crucial for creating immersive audio experiences in virtual environments, games, simulations, and multimedia applications. The ability to accurately simulate how sound interacts with virtual spaces adds depth and realism to auditory experiences, contributing significantly to the overall sense of presence and immersion. As technology continues to evolve, we can anticipate even more sophisticated real-time reverberation solutions that push the boundaries of audio realism in the digital realm.

Section 10.3: Advanced Audio Simulation

Advanced audio simulation techniques are essential for creating rich, immersive soundscapes in various applications, including games, virtual reality (VR), augmented reality (AR), and simulations. These techniques go beyond basic audio playback and aim to replicate real-world audio phenomena to enhance the overall user experience.

1. Physical Modeling:

One approach to advanced audio simulation is physical modeling. This technique simulates the behavior of real-world acoustic objects, such as instruments or environments. For example, in a virtual drum kit, physical modeling can simulate how the drumhead vibrates and how sound waves propagate through the virtual space.

2. Wave-Based Simulation:

Wave-based simulation is another powerful technique for advanced audio. It involves simulating sound waves as they propagate through a virtual environment. This can capture complex interactions, including reflections, diffraction, and interference, resulting in highly realistic audio experiences.

3. Dynamic Environmental Audio:

In games and VR/AR applications, audio should respond dynamically to changes in the virtual environment. For instance, as a character moves from a quiet indoor space to a noisy outdoor area, the audio simulation should adapt accordingly, mimicking how sound behaves in the real world.

4. Sound Propagation:

Advanced audio simulations often incorporate sound propagation algorithms. These algorithms calculate how sound travels through different materials and spaces, accounting for factors like absorption, reflection, and scattering. This contributes to the authenticity of the audio experience.

5. Binaural Audio:

Binaural audio is a key component of immersive audio. It simulates how we perceive sound in 3D space using two ears. By providing distinct audio signals to each ear, binaural audio enhances spatial awareness and immersion, making it feel like sound is coming from specific directions.

6. Real-time DSP Effects:

Real-time digital signal processing (DSP) effects are often applied in advanced audio simulation to modify audio on the fly. These effects can include reverberation, echo, filtering, and more, all of which contribute to a more realistic and engaging audio experience.

7. HRTF (Head-Related Transfer Function):

HRTF is a critical element of binaural audio. It accounts for the unique filtering and time delays that occur as sound waves interact with the listener's head and ears. Precise HRTF data is necessary for accurate 3D audio positioning.

8. Audio Occlusion and Diffraction:

In complex environments, audio can be occluded (blocked) or diffracted (bent) by objects. Advanced audio simulations take these phenomena into account, ensuring that audio behaves realistically even when objects obstruct sound sources.

9. Dynamic Mixing and Spatialization:

As the virtual environment changes, audio mixing and spatialization adapt accordingly. This ensures that the user hears sounds from the correct direction and that audio levels are adjusted realistically based on distance and obstacles.

10. Performance Considerations:

Implementing advanced audio simulation can be computationally intensive. Developers must strike a balance between realism and performance, optimizing code and leveraging hardware acceleration where available.

11. Middleware and Audio Engines:

Many game engines and audio middleware solutions offer advanced audio simulation tools and libraries. These tools simplify the implementation of complex audio effects and interactions.

12. User Experience Enhancement:

Ultimately, the goal of advanced audio simulation is to enhance the user experience by making virtual environments feel more immersive and true to life. Well-executed audio simulations can significantly contribute to the overall sense of presence and engagement in VR, AR, and gaming.

In summary, advanced audio simulation techniques are crucial for creating immersive, realistic audio experiences in digital environments. Whether it's replicating the physics of sound, simulating wave propagation, or providing dynamic and spatially accurate audio, these techniques play a vital role in enhancing user immersion and engagement in interactive applications. As hardware and software continue to advance, we can expect even more sophisticated and convincing audio simulations in the future.

Section 10.4: Sound Propagation in Complex Environments

Sound propagation in complex virtual environments is a critical aspect of creating immersive audio experiences. Whether in gaming, virtual reality (VR), or architectural simulations, accurately simulating how sound travels and interacts with various elements adds realism and depth to the audio landscape. This section delves into techniques for simulating sound propagation in complex digital spaces.

1. Geometric Acoustics:

Geometric acoustics is a foundational concept in sound propagation modeling. It involves tracing sound rays as they bounce off surfaces and interact with objects. This approach is suitable for simulating high-frequency sounds, like reflections and echoes, which are essential for creating realistic audio environments.

2. Ray Tracing:

Ray tracing is commonly used to calculate sound propagation in complex environments. By tracing sound rays and simulating their interactions with surfaces and materials, it becomes possible to generate accurate sound reflections and diffractions. Ray tracing also allows for the calculation of sound occlusion, where objects block or alter sound waves.

3. Materials and Absorption:

Different materials absorb and reflect sound differently. In complex audio simulations, it's crucial to consider the acoustic properties of materials. Materials can be classified based on their absorption coefficients, which dictate how much sound energy they absorb. Incorporating these properties into simulations ensures that audio behaves realistically when interacting with various surfaces.

4. Reverberation:

Reverberation is a vital component of sound propagation. It occurs when sound waves reflect multiple times in an environment, creating a sense of space. Simulating reverberation accurately involves modeling the number of reflections, their timing, and how they affect the audio. This is particularly important for large, open spaces where echoes are prominent.

5. Convolution and Impulse Responses:

Convolution is a mathematical operation used in sound propagation simulations. It involves combining an audio signal with an impulse response of the environment. This process accurately represents how sound interacts with the environment and produces realistic spatial audio effects.

6. Dynamic Environments:

In interactive applications, environments often change dynamically. Sound propagation simulations must adapt in real-time to reflect these changes. For example, if a door is opened or closed, it should affect how sound travels through a space.

7. Computational Complexity:

Simulating sound propagation in complex environments can be computationally demanding. Developers must optimize algorithms and leverage hardware acceleration to achieve real-time performance, especially in VR and gaming scenarios where low latency is crucial.

8. Middleware and Audio Engines:

Many game engines and audio middleware solutions offer tools and libraries for sound propagation simulations. These solutions simplify the implementation of complex acoustic effects and interactions.

9. Real-time Ray Tracing:

With advancements in hardware, real-time ray tracing is becoming increasingly feasible. Real-time ray tracing can greatly enhance the accuracy of sound propagation simulations by simulating complex interactions between sound and the environment.

10. Immersive Audio Experiences:

Accurate sound propagation in complex environments contributes to creating immersive audio experiences. Whether it's exploring ancient dungeons in a game or walking through a virtual architectural space, realistic sound propagation enhances the sense of presence and immersion.

In conclusion, sound propagation in complex virtual environments is a multidisciplinary field that combines physics, mathematics, and computer science to create realistic audio experiences. Techniques like ray tracing, materials modeling, and real-time adaptation are crucial for simulating sound in dynamic and interactive digital spaces. As hardware continues to advance, we can expect even more convincing and immersive audio simulations in the future, further enhancing the overall quality of virtual and augmented reality experiences.

Section 10.5: Audio Shaders and Processing

Audio shaders and processing techniques play a vital role in shaping the auditory experience within digital environments. These techniques allow developers to create unique and dynamic audio effects, enhancing immersion and realism in interactive applications. In this section, we explore the concepts and applications of audio shaders and processing.

1. Audio Shaders Overview:

Audio shaders are programs that manipulate audio data in real-time. They are analogous to graphics shaders but focus on sound generation, manipulation, and spatialization. Audio shaders are commonly used in gaming, VR, and multimedia applications to create dynamic and responsive audio experiences.

2. Dynamic Sound Generation:

Audio shaders can generate sound on-the-fly, allowing for procedurally generated audio effects. This is useful for creating sounds that respond to in-game events or environmental changes. For example, footsteps on different surfaces or the sound of a virtual object colliding with others.

3. Real-time Filters and Effects:

Audio shaders can apply real-time filters and effects to audio sources. This includes effects like reverb, equalization, modulation, and convolution. These effects shape the audio's characteristics, making it suitable for various scenarios and environments.

4. Spatial Audio:

Spatialization is a key aspect of audio shaders. It involves placing sounds in a 3D space to create a sense of direction and distance. Audio shaders can simulate how sound interacts with the environment, producing realistic 3D audio experiences in VR and gaming.

5. Doppler Effect and Velocity:

Implementing the Doppler effect in audio shaders allows for realistic sound changes as objects or characters move through the environment. As objects approach or recede from the listener, their audio pitch and volume change accordingly.

6. Environmental Audio:

Audio shaders can account for the surroundings. For example, they can simulate how sound travels differently in open spaces, narrow corridors, or reverberant chambers. This contributes to a more authentic and immersive experience.

7. Dynamic Mixing and Balancing:

In interactive applications, audio shaders dynamically adjust the mix and balance of sound sources based on player actions. This ensures that the most relevant sounds are emphasized, enhancing gameplay or storytelling.

8. Audio Synthesis:

Audio shaders can synthesize complex sounds, including music and ambient audio, in real-time. This is valuable for generating adaptive soundtracks that respond to the game's progression and events.

9. Performance Optimization:

Optimizing audio shaders is essential for maintaining a smooth and responsive experience. Developers must consider factors like CPU usage and memory management to ensure that audio processing doesn't introduce performance bottlenecks.

10. Integration with Game Engines:

Many game engines provide support for audio shaders and real-time audio processing. Developers can leverage these tools to streamline the implementation of advanced audio effects.

11. Cross-platform Compatibility:

Ensuring that audio shaders work consistently across different platforms and hardware configurations is crucial for delivering a uniform experience to players and users.

12. Future Trends:

As hardware capabilities continue to advance, the possibilities for audio shaders expand. Realistic and dynamic audio is becoming an increasingly important aspect of immersive experiences in gaming, VR, and AR.

In summary, audio shaders and processing techniques are fundamental for creating engaging and realistic auditory experiences in digital environments. Whether used for spatial audio, dynamic sound generation, or environmental audio effects, audio shaders enhance the overall immersion and quality of interactive applications. As technology continues to evolve, audio will play an even more significant role in shaping the future of digital experiences.

Chapter 11: Procedural Generation Techniques

Section 11.1: Procedural Modelling and Texturing

Procedural generation is a powerful technique used in various aspects of computer graphics and game development. In this section, we'll explore procedural modeling and texturing, focusing on generating complex 3D models and textures algorithmically. Procedural generation offers several advantages, such as reducing storage requirements, enabling dynamic content generation, and enhancing realism.

Procedural Modeling

Procedural modeling involves creating 3D models through algorithms rather than traditional manual modeling techniques. This approach is especially useful when you need a large number of similar objects or want to achieve a natural, organic look.

One common procedural modeling technique is **L-Systems** (Lindenmayer Systems), which uses a set of rules to iteratively replace components of a model. L-Systems are frequently used to generate branching structures like trees, plants, or complex architectural designs.

Here's a simplified example of an L-System for generating a fractal tree:

```
# Pseudocode for a simple L-System

axiom = "X"
```

```python
rules = {

"X": "F-[[X]+X]+F[+FX]-X",

"F": "FF"

}

iterations = 4

result = axiom

for _ in range(iterations):

next_result = ""

for char in result:

next_result += rules.get(char, char)

result = next_result

# Interpret the result and render the 3D model
```

Procedural Texturing

Procedural texturing allows you to generate textures on-the-fly based on mathematical functions and patterns. This technique can be used to create various surface effects, including marble, wood, clouds, and more.

One commonly used procedural texturing method is **Perlin noise**, which generates natural-looking patterns. Perlin noise can be scaled, rotated, and combined to create a wide range of textures.

Here's an example of generating Perlin noise in Python using the noise library:

```
import noise

# Generate a Perlin noise texture

width, height = 512, 512

scale = 100.0

octaves = 6

persistence = 0.5

lacunarity = 2.0

world = noise.Perlin(octaves=octaves, persistence=persistence, lacunarity=lacunarity, repeatx=1024, repeaty=1024, base=42)

image = noise.Image(width, height, scale=scale, world=world)

image.save_to_file("perlin_noise.png")
```

Procedural texturing is beneficial for creating infinite and unique textures for terrains, landscapes, and other surfaces in games and simulations.

In summary, procedural modeling and texturing offer powerful tools for creating complex and dynamic content in computer graphics and game development. These techniques can significantly enhance the visual richness and diversity of virtual worlds while minimizing storage requirements.

Section 11.2: Infinite Worlds and Fractal Geometry

Infinite worlds and fractal geometry are fascinating topics in the realm of procedural content generation. They allow game developers and artists to create expansive and varied virtual landscapes, environments, and structures without the need for extensive manual design. In this section, we'll delve into the concept of generating infinite worlds using fractal geometry and explore their applications in video games, simulations, and virtual environments.

Understanding Fractal Geometry

Fractal geometry is a branch of mathematics that deals with complex, self-replicating patterns. These patterns are characterized by their self-similarity at different scales. One of the most famous examples of a fractal is the **Mandelbrot set**, a visual representation of a mathematical equation. The Mandelbrot set exhibits intricate and infinitely detailed patterns as you zoom in, revealing smaller copies of the whole structure.

Fractals are used in various fields, including computer graphics, due to their ability to generate complex and visually interesting shapes efficiently. In procedural content generation, fractals can be employed to create natural landscapes, terrain, and other intricate structures.

Generating Infinite Worlds

The concept of infinite worlds in video games is particularly appealing because it allows players to explore vast virtual realms without running into boundaries. Infinite worlds are often employed in sandbox-style games, survival games, and exploration-focused titles.

One common approach to generating infinite worlds is to use a **noise function**. Perlin noise, as mentioned in the previous section, is a popular choice. By carefully controlling the parameters of the noise function, you can create landscapes with various features like mountains, valleys, and rivers.

Here's a simplified example of generating a heightmap for an infinite terrain using Perlin noise in Python:

```python
import noise

import numpy as np

import matplotlib.pyplot as plt

# Generate a heightmap using Perlin noise

width, height = 512, 512

scale = 100.0

octaves = 6

persistence = 0.5

lacunarity = 2.0

world = noise.Perlin(octaves=octaves, persistence=persistence,
lacunarity=lacunarity, repeatx=1024, repeaty=1024, base=42)

# Create a 2D array to store the heightmap

heightmap = np.zeros((height, width))

for y in range(height):

for x in range(width):

heightmap[y][x] = world.noise2(x / scale, y / scale)

# Visualize the heightmap

plt.imshow(heightmap, cmap='terrain', origin='lower')

plt.colorbar()
```

plt.show()

This heightmap can serve as the foundation for generating a vast and continuous terrain in a game world.

Infinite worlds and fractal geometry open up exciting possibilities for game developers to create expansive, ever-changing, and captivating virtual environments. These techniques enable the generation of terrain, landscapes, and structures that extend indefinitely, offering players endless opportunities for exploration and discovery.

Section 11.3: Advanced Terrain Generation

Advanced terrain generation is a critical aspect of many video games and simulations, especially those that aim to provide realistic and immersive virtual worlds. In this section, we will explore techniques and algorithms used in the creation of complex and visually stunning terrain, enabling developers to craft engaging environments for their games and applications.

Heightmap-Based Terrain Generation

One of the most common approaches to terrain generation is heightmap-based techniques. A heightmap is a two-dimensional grid of values where each value represents the height of a point on the terrain. By manipulating these height values, developers can create a variety of terrain features such as mountains, valleys, plateaus, and more.

A well-known algorithm for generating realistic terrain using heightmaps is the **Diamond-Square Algorithm**. This algorithm works by recursively subdividing a square into four smaller squares, perturbing the center point's height based on nearby heights. The process continues iteratively, producing terrain with fractal-like features.

Here's a simplified example of generating terrain using the Diamond-Square Algorithm in Python:

```python
import numpy as np

def diamond_square(heightmap, x1, y1, x2, y2, roughness):

    # Calculate midpoint

    mx = (x1 + x2) // 2

    my = (y1 + y2) // 2

    # Diamond step

    heightmap[mx, my] = (heightmap[x1, y1] + heightmap[x1, y2] +
    heightmap[x2, y1] + heightmap[x2, y2]) / 4 +
    np.random.uniform(-roughness, roughness)

    # Square step

    heightmap[mx, y1] = (heightmap[x1, y1] + heightmap[x2, y1] +
    heightmap[mx, my]) / 3 + np.random.uniform(-roughness,
    roughness)

    heightmap[mx, y2] = (heightmap[x1, y2] + heightmap[x2, y2] +
    heightmap[mx, my]) / 3 + np.random.uniform(-roughness,
    roughness)

    heightmap[x1, my] = (heightmap[x1, y1] + heightmap[x1, y2] +
    heightmap[mx, my]) / 3 + np.random.uniform(-roughness,
    roughness)
```

```
heightmap[x2, my] = (heightmap[x2, y1] + heightmap[x2, y2] +
heightmap[mx, my]) / 3 + np.random.uniform(-roughness,
roughness)

if mx - x1 > 1:

diamond_square(heightmap, x1, y1, mx, my, roughness)

diamond_square(heightmap, mx, y1, x2, my, roughness)

diamond_square(heightmap, x1, my, mx, y2, roughness)

diamond_square(heightmap, mx, my, x2, y2, roughness)

# Example usage

size = 9

heightmap = np.zeros((size, size))

roughness = 0.5

diamond_square(heightmap, 0, 0, size - 1, size - 1, roughness)
```

Procedural Noise-Based Terrain

Procedural noise functions, such as Perlin noise and simplex noise,
are powerful tools for generating terrain. These functions can
produce a wide range of natural-looking landscapes, including
rugged mountains, rolling hills, and flat plains. By varying the
parameters of the noise functions, developers can control the
terrain's characteristics, such as its roughness, scale, and features.

Here's a simple example of generating terrain using Perlin noise in
Python:

```
import noise
```

```python
import numpy as np

import matplotlib.pyplot as plt

# Parameters

width, height = 512, 512

scale = 100.0

octaves = 6

persistence = 0.5

lacunarity = 2.0

# Create a 2D array to store the heightmap

heightmap = np.zeros((height, width))

# Generate terrain using Perlin noise

for y in range(height):

for x in range(width):

heightmap[y][x] = noise.pnoise2(x / scale, y / scale, octaves=octaves,
persistence=persistence, lacunarity=lacunarity, repeatx=1024,
repeaty=1024, base=42)

# Visualize the heightmap

plt.imshow(heightmap, cmap='terrain', origin='lower')

plt.colorbar()

plt.show()
```

Both heightmap-based and procedural noise-based terrain generation techniques offer significant flexibility and are widely used in the game development industry. These methods allow developers to create diverse and captivating terrains that enhance the overall gaming experience.

Section 11.4: Procedural Animation

Procedural animation is a powerful approach used in video game development and computer graphics to create lifelike and dynamic animations without relying on pre-authored keyframes. This section explores the concept of procedural animation and provides insights into how it can be applied to various aspects of game development, including character movement, object interactions, and environmental effects.

Principles of Procedural Animation

Procedural animation is driven by algorithms and mathematical models, making it adaptable and responsive to in-game events and player interactions. Unlike traditional animation techniques, where animations are manually created and stored, procedural animation generates animations in real-time based on the current state of the game.

Here are some key principles of procedural animation:

1. **Physics-Based Simulations:** Many procedural animations leverage physics simulations to achieve realism. For example, character movements can be simulated using ragdoll physics for natural-looking reactions to external forces.

2. **Inverse Kinematics (IK):** IK solvers are used to determine the joint configurations required to reach a specific target.

This is commonly used in character animation for tasks like reaching for objects or maintaining balance.

3. **Procedural Deformation:** Procedural animation can deform character models and objects dynamically. For instance, a character's body shape may change realistically when it interacts with the environment, such as when pressing against a wall.

4. **Behavior Trees:** Procedural animation often involves behavior trees, a way to define complex behaviors by combining simple actions and decisions. This allows for dynamic character responses to different situations.

Applications of Procedural Animation

1. Character Animation:

Procedural animation is frequently used to create lifelike character movements. By simulating physical constraints, characters can respond realistically to their environment. For example, characters can stumble when walking on uneven terrain, maintain balance when pushed, or exhibit natural limb movements.

```
// Example of procedural character animation in Unity using IK

void Update() {

// Calculate IK target position based on player input

Vector3 targetPosition = CalculateIKTarget();

// Set IK target position for character's hand

animator.SetIKPosition(AvatarIKGoal.RightHand, targetPosition);

}
```

2. Environmental Effects:

Procedural animation extends beyond characters to environmental effects. For instance, swaying vegetation, rippling water surfaces, and dynamic weather patterns can be achieved through procedural techniques. These animations respond to in-game factors like wind, rain, or player interactions.

```
# Example of procedural water animation using sine waves

def UpdateWater():

time = GetCurrentTime()

waterSurfaceVertices = GetWaterSurfaceVertices()

for vertex in waterSurfaceVertices:

# Apply sine wave deformation to simulate water ripples

vertex.position.y  =  Mathf.Sin(time  *  vertex.frequency  +
vertex.phase) * vertex.amplitude
```

3. Object Interactions:

Procedural animation is also used to generate object interactions. For instance, when a character pushes or lifts an object, the object's response is computed procedurally based on physics simulations and object properties.

```
// Example of procedural object interaction using Unity's physics engine

void    PushObject(Rigidbody    objectRigidbody,    Vector3
pushDirection, float pushForce) {
```

```
// Apply force to the object's rigidbody to simulate pushing

objectRigidbody.AddForce(pushDirection        *        pushForce,
ForceMode.Impulse);

}
```

Benefits and Challenges

Procedural animation offers several advantages, including increased realism, adaptability to various scenarios, and reduced reliance on pre-made animations. However, it also presents challenges in terms of computational complexity and fine-tuning to achieve desired results. Game developers often strike a balance between procedural and pre-authored animations to achieve the best outcome for their projects.

In summary, procedural animation is a valuable tool in game development, enabling dynamic and lifelike animations for characters, objects, and environmental effects. Its use extends beyond games and is increasingly applied in various industries, including simulation, virtual reality, and augmented reality, to create immersive and interactive experiences.

Section 11.5: Dynamic Story and World Generation

Dynamic story and world generation is a game development technique that involves creating procedural and adaptive content to enhance player experiences. Instead of relying solely on static, pre-designed game worlds and narratives, dynamic generation algorithms allow for on-the-fly creation of game content, making each playthrough unique. This section explores the concept of dynamic story and world generation and its applications in video game development.

Procedural Content Generation (PCG)

Procedural content generation is at the core of dynamic story and world generation. PCG involves creating game content, such as levels, environments, characters, items, and narratives, algorithmically rather than manually. This approach has several advantages:

1. **Replayability:** Procedurally generated content ensures that no two playthroughs are exactly the same, leading to increased replayability.
2. **Scalability:** Game worlds can be generated to fit the player's progress or exploration, adapting to their choices and actions.
3. **Efficiency:** PCG reduces the time and effort required to design and create large, complex game worlds.

World Generation Example:

```
# Example of procedural terrain generation using Perlin noise

def GenerateTerrain(width, height):

terrain = []

for x in range(width):

terrain_column = []

for y in range(height):

# Generate terrain height using Perlin noise
```

```
height_value = PerlinNoise(x * 0.1, y * 0.1)

terrain_column.append(height_value)

terrain.append(terrain_column)

return terrain
```

Dynamic Storytelling

Dynamic storytelling involves adapting the game's narrative and plot based on player choices, actions, and progress. It allows for non-linear storytelling, where the player's decisions influence the direction and outcome of the story. Dynamic storytelling systems often use branching narratives, where each choice leads to different story arcs and outcomes.

Branching Narrative Example:

```
// Example of branching dialogue system in a game

void StartConversation(NPC npc) {

DialogueNode currentNode = npc.GetStartingNode();

while (currentNode != null) {

DisplayDialogue(currentNode.Text);

List<DialogueOption> options = currentNode.GetOptions();

// Wait for player input to choose a dialogue option

int selectedOption = WaitForPlayerInput(options);

// Set the next dialogue node based on the player's choice
```

```
currentNode = options[selectedOption].NextNode;

    }

}
```

Challenges and Considerations

While dynamic story and world generation offer exciting possibilities, they come with challenges:

1. **Narrative Coherence:** Maintaining a coherent and engaging narrative can be challenging when the story adapts to player choices.
2. **Balancing Difficulty:** Procedurally generated game content must be balanced to ensure fair and enjoyable gameplay.
3. **Player Agency:** Giving players meaningful choices and consequences can be complex to implement effectively.
4. **Performance:** Generating content in real-time can impact game performance, requiring careful optimization.

Applications

Dynamic story and world generation techniques are prevalent in roguelike games, open-world exploration titles, and role-playing games (RPGs). These systems allow developers to create expansive, adaptive game worlds and engaging narratives that respond to player actions. Additionally, they can be used in educational and simulation games to create dynamic learning experiences.

In conclusion, dynamic story and world generation are powerful tools in game development that enhance replayability and player engagement. When implemented effectively, these techniques create immersive, ever-changing game worlds and narratives that captivate players and offer unique experiences with each playthrough.

Chapter 12: Mixed Reality Rendering

Section 12.1: Merging VR and AR Techniques

Mixed Reality (MR) is a technology that combines elements of both Virtual Reality (VR) and Augmented Reality (AR) to create immersive and interactive experiences. In this section, we will explore the merging of VR and AR techniques to develop applications that seamlessly blend the digital and physical worlds.

Understanding VR and AR

Before delving into mixed reality, it's essential to understand VR and AR:

- **Virtual Reality (VR):** VR creates a fully immersive digital environment that replaces the physical world. Users wear VR headsets that cover their field of vision, and they can interact with the virtual world using motion controllers.

- **Augmented Reality (AR):** AR overlays digital content onto the real world. Users typically view AR content through devices like smartphones, tablets, or AR glasses. AR enhances the real-world experience by adding digital information or objects.

Mixed Reality Concepts

Mixed Reality bridges the gap between VR and AR by allowing digital and physical elements to coexist and interact. Here are some key concepts:

1. **Spatial Mapping:** MR devices use sensors to map the physical environment in real-time. This mapping enables the placement of digital objects in the physical world.
2. **Holograms:** Digital objects in MR are often referred to as holograms. Holograms can be static or dynamic and interact with the user or the environment.
3. **Gesture and Voice Control:** Users can interact with holograms using gestures, voice commands, or physical controllers.
4. **Anchors:** Anchors are points in the physical environment where holograms can be attached. They help maintain the spatial consistency of holograms.

Development Platforms

To develop MR applications, developers can leverage various platforms and technologies:

- **Microsoft HoloLens:** HoloLens is a popular MR headset developed by Microsoft. It runs on Windows Mixed Reality, a platform that allows developers to create MR applications.

- **Unity3D:** Unity is a widely-used game engine that supports MR development. It offers tools and plugins for creating holographic applications.

- **ARKit and ARCore:** Apple's ARKit and Google's ARCore are AR development frameworks that can be extended to support MR features.

Use Cases

The merging of VR and AR techniques opens up exciting possibilities across industries:

- **Gaming:** MR gaming experiences can blend real-world elements with digital gameplay, creating immersive and interactive scenarios.

- **Education:** MR can enhance educational content by overlaying 3D models, simulations, and information on physical objects.

- **Remote Assistance:** MR enables experts to provide remote assistance by visualizing digital annotations or instructions within the user's environment.

- **Design and Engineering:** Architects and engineers can use MR to visualize and interact with 3D models in real-world contexts, facilitating design and prototyping.

Challenges

While MR offers promising opportunities, it also poses challenges:

- **Hardware Limitations:** MR devices are still evolving, and limitations in field of view, weight, and battery life need to be addressed.

- **Content Creation:** Creating compelling MR content requires a combination of 3D modeling, programming, and UX design skills.

- **User Interaction:** Designing intuitive and natural interactions with holograms can be complex.

In conclusion, the merging of VR and AR techniques into Mixed Reality has the potential to revolutionize how we interact with digital information and experiences. As MR hardware and development tools continue to advance, we can expect to see a broader range of applications that seamlessly blend the digital and physical worlds.

Section 12.2: Real-time Object Tracking

Real-time object tracking is a fundamental component of mixed reality (MR) rendering, enabling MR devices to understand and interact with physical objects in the user's environment. In this section, we'll explore the concepts and techniques behind real-time object tracking in MR applications.

Object Recognition and Tracking

Object tracking involves identifying and following specific objects in the real world. MR devices use computer vision algorithms and sensors, such as cameras, to achieve this. Here's a high-level overview of the process:

1. **Object Detection:** The device's camera captures the user's surroundings, and computer vision algorithms analyze the video feed to detect objects. This detection is often based on patterns, shapes, or predefined markers.
2. **Object Identification:** Once an object is detected, it's identified using techniques like feature matching, machine learning, or marker recognition. This step determines what the object is and provides context for interaction.
3. **Tracking:** After identification, the device continuously tracks the object's position and orientation in real-time. This tracking information is crucial for rendering digital

content that interacts with the object.

Marker-based Tracking

One common approach to object tracking in MR is marker-based tracking. It involves using physical markers, such as QR codes or fiducial markers, that are easily distinguishable by the MR device's camera. These markers serve as reference points for tracking.

Here's a simplified example of marker-based tracking using Python and OpenCV:

```python
import cv2

import numpy as np

# Load a marker image

marker_image = cv2.imread('marker.png', cv2.IMREAD_GRAYSCALE)

# Initialize the camera

cap = cv2.VideoCapture(0)

while True:

    ret, frame = cap.read()

    # Detect the marker in the camera frame

    detector = cv2.ARUCO_MIP_25h7

    parameters = cv2.aruco.DetectorParameters_create()

    corners, ids, _ = cv2.aruco.detectMarkers(frame, detector, parameters=parameters)
```

```python
if ids is not None:

# Marker detected, draw a bounding box around it

for i in range(len(ids)):

cv2.aruco.drawDetectedMarkers(frame, corners)

cv2.imshow('Object Tracking', frame)

if cv2.waitKey(1) & 0xFF == ord('q'):

break

cap.release()

cv2.destroyAllWindows()
```

In this example, we use the ArUco library, a popular marker-based tracking library in OpenCV, to detect and draw markers in real-time camera frames.

Markerless Tracking

While marker-based tracking is effective, markerless tracking is a more advanced technique that doesn't rely on predefined markers. Instead, it tracks objects based on their unique features, like shapes, textures, or distinct visual characteristics.

Markerless tracking often involves techniques like feature detection and matching, structure from motion (SfM), and simultaneous localization and mapping (SLAM). These techniques enable MR devices to track a wider range of objects and scenes, making the tracking experience more versatile.

Challenges and Considerations

Real-time object tracking in MR comes with several challenges:

- **Accuracy:** Ensuring accurate and robust tracking, especially in complex or dynamic environments, is a significant challenge.

- **Latency:** Achieving low-latency tracking is crucial for a smooth MR experience.

- **Computational Resources:** Object tracking can be computationally intensive, requiring powerful processors and efficient algorithms.

- **Privacy:** Handling and processing camera data raise privacy concerns that need to be addressed.

In conclusion, real-time object tracking is a fundamental capability in mixed reality applications, enabling the seamless integration of digital content with the physical world. Marker-based and markerless tracking techniques play essential roles in creating immersive MR experiences, and ongoing advancements in computer vision and hardware are continually improving the state of object tracking in MR.

Section 12.3: Scene Reconstruction from Video

Scene reconstruction from video is a critical aspect of mixed reality (MR) rendering. It involves creating a digital representation of the user's physical environment, allowing MR devices to interact with and augment the real world. In this section, we'll explore the principles and techniques behind scene reconstruction from video.

Understanding Scene Reconstruction

Scene reconstruction aims to build a 3D model of the environment by analyzing video footage. This process typically involves the following steps:

1. **Camera Pose Estimation:** MR devices use multiple cameras or sensors to capture the environment from different viewpoints. These cameras need to be calibrated and synchronized. Algorithms estimate the precise position and orientation of each camera, known as the camera pose, in relation to a common coordinate system.
2. **Feature Extraction:** The video frames are analyzed to identify distinctive features, such as corners, edges, or key points. These features serve as reference points for tracking and aligning frames.
3. **Depth Sensing:** To create a 3D model, depth information is essential. Some MR devices use structured light, time-of-flight sensors, or stereo vision to estimate the depth of objects in the scene.
4. **Visual Odometry:** Visual odometry techniques track the movement of the cameras over time. This information is used to refine the camera poses and build a more accurate 3D model.
5. **Point Cloud Generation:** Once camera poses and depth information are known, a point cloud is generated. This point cloud represents the 3D positions of objects in the scene.
6. **Mesh Generation:** The point cloud is often converted into a mesh, which defines the surfaces and geometry of objects in the environment. Textures and colors from the video frames can also be mapped onto the mesh.
7. **Rendering and Integration:** The 3D model is integrated

into the MR environment. Digital objects can interact
with the physical world based on the reconstructed scene.

SLAM (Simultaneous Localization and Mapping)

One of the fundamental techniques used in scene reconstruction is
SLAM. SLAM algorithms simultaneously estimate the camera poses
and create a map of the environment. Visual SLAM relies on visual
data (camera images), while RGB-D SLAM combines visual data
with depth information.

Here's a simplified example of visual SLAM using Python and the
OpenCV library:

```python
import cv2

import numpy as np

# Initialize SLAM

slam = cv2.SFMDetector_create()

map_points = []

trajectory = []

# Process video frames

cap = cv2.VideoCapture('video.mp4')

while True:

ret, frame = cap.read()

if not ret:

break
```

```
# Process the frame and update SLAM

gray = cv2.cvtColor(frame, cv2.COLOR_BGR2GRAY)

keypoints, descriptors = slam.detectAndCompute(gray, None)

map_points.append((keypoints, descriptors))

# Update camera pose and map

pose = slam.update(map_points[-1], frame)

trajectory.append(pose)

# Render the reconstructed scene

# (Render digital objects and overlay on the video frame)

# Display the frame

cv2.imshow('Scene Reconstruction', frame)

if cv2.waitKey(1) & 0xFF == ord('q'):

break

cap.release()

cv2.destroyAllWindows()
```

This example uses the Structure from Motion (SfM) detector in OpenCV to perform visual SLAM and reconstruct the scene from a video file.

Challenges and Considerations

Scene reconstruction from video presents several challenges:

- **Scale:** Ensuring accurate scale in the reconstructed model is critical. Errors in scale can lead to misalignment of digital objects with the physical environment.

- **Dynamic Objects:** Handling dynamic objects and changes in the environment is a challenge. Advanced techniques use object tracking and dynamic mesh updates to address this issue.

- **Computational Demands:** Scene reconstruction can be computationally intensive, requiring substantial processing power and memory.

- **Sensor Calibration:** Accurate calibration of cameras and depth sensors is crucial for precise scene reconstruction.

In conclusion, scene reconstruction from video is a complex but essential component of mixed reality rendering. It enables MR devices to create immersive experiences by seamlessly blending digital content with the physical world. Ongoing advancements in computer vision and sensor technology continue to enhance the accuracy and capabilities of scene reconstruction in MR applications.

Section 12.4: Real-world Lighting in AR

Real-world lighting is a crucial aspect of creating immersive augmented reality (AR) experiences. To convincingly merge virtual objects with the physical world, AR applications must accurately simulate and interact with real-world lighting conditions. In this section, we'll delve into the challenges and techniques involved in achieving realistic lighting in AR.

Challenges in Real-world Lighting

1. **Ambient Light Estimation:** One of the primary challenges is estimating the ambient light in the physical environment. AR devices equipped with sensors like photodiodes or light sensors can measure the intensity and color of ambient light. This information is essential for adjusting the appearance of virtual objects.

2. **Directional Light Sources:** Real-world lighting often involves multiple light sources with varying directions and intensities, such as sunlight, lamps, or reflections. Capturing these dynamic sources and accurately illuminating virtual objects is a complex task.

3. **Shadow Interaction:** Shadows play a critical role in perceiving depth and realism. Virtual objects must cast realistic shadows that interact with the environment and other objects.

4. **Material Reflectance:** Virtual objects should respond to light in a manner consistent with their material properties. This includes considerations for materials like metal, glass, and matte surfaces.

5. **Color and Tone Matching:** Achieving a seamless blend between real and virtual objects requires matching the color, tone, and contrast of virtual elements with the physical environment.

Techniques for Real-world Lighting

1. **Image-Based Lighting (IBL):** IBL is a popular technique used to capture the environment's lighting information in a form that can be used to illuminate virtual objects. This involves capturing high-dynamic-range (HDR) images or cube maps of the surroundings and then using this data to

light the virtual scene.

2. **Physically Based Rendering (PBR):** PBR techniques model the interaction between light and materials more accurately, resulting in realistic shading and reflections. PBR materials store information about how they respond to light, allowing virtual objects to blend seamlessly with the real world.

3. **Environment Probe:** AR applications can use environment probes, which capture the lighting conditions from the device's surroundings. These probes help simulate reflections and lighting on virtual objects.

4. **Shadow Mapping:** To create realistic shadows, shadow mapping techniques are employed. Depth information from the real world is used to cast shadows onto virtual objects. Advanced techniques like Percentage Closer Soft Shadows (PCSS) enhance shadow realism.

5. **Real-time Global Illumination (GI):** Some AR platforms offer real-time GI solutions that simulate indirect lighting and color bleeding. These techniques further enhance the realism of virtual objects by accounting for the environment's illumination.

6. **Dynamic Tone Mapping:** To match the tone and contrast of virtual and real elements, dynamic tone mapping adjusts the virtual scene's appearance based on ambient light conditions.

Here's a simplified code example in Unity using AR Foundation and ARKit to demonstrate real-world lighting in an AR scene:

```
using UnityEngine;

using UnityEngine.XR.ARSubsystems;

using UnityEngine.XR.ARFoundation;
```

```csharp
public class RealWorldLighting : MonoBehaviour
{
[SerializeField] private ARCameraManager arCameraManager;
[SerializeField] private Light directionalLight;
private void OnEnable()
{
arCameraManager.frameReceived += OnFrameReceived;
}
private void OnDisable()
{
arCameraManager.frameReceived -= OnFrameReceived;
}
private void OnFrameReceived(ARCameraFrameEventArgs eventArgs)
{
// Access ambient light intensity and color
float lightIntensity = eventArgs.lightEstimation.averageBrightness;
Color lightColor = eventArgs.lightEstimation.colorCorrection;
// Update directional light intensity and color
directionalLight.intensity = lightIntensity;
directionalLight.color = lightColor;
```

```
}

}
```

This Unity script adjusts the intensity and color of a directional light in response to real-world ambient lighting conditions, helping virtual objects appear more realistically lit in AR.

In conclusion, achieving real-world lighting in AR is essential for creating convincing and immersive augmented reality experiences. By accurately capturing and simulating the lighting environment, AR applications can seamlessly blend virtual and physical elements, enhancing the overall realism and user experience.

Section 12.5: Physical and Virtual Interactions

Interactions between physical and virtual elements are at the heart of mixed reality (MR) experiences. In this section, we will explore the various ways in which physical and virtual entities can interact, creating immersive and engaging MR scenarios.

Types of Interactions

1. **Spatial Tracking:** MR devices equipped with sensors, such as cameras and depth sensors, can track the user's movements and the position of physical objects in real-time. This spatial tracking enables precise alignment of virtual objects with the physical environment.

2. **Gesture Recognition:** Many MR systems support gesture recognition, allowing users to interact with virtual content using hand gestures. Common gestures include tapping, swiping, and pinching, which can be used to manipulate virtual objects or activate functions.

3. **Voice Commands:** Voice recognition technology is often integrated into MR headsets. Users can issue voice commands to control virtual elements, perform actions, or retrieve information, enhancing the hands-free nature of the experience.

4. **Haptic Feedback:** Haptic feedback devices provide tactile sensations to users, enhancing the sense of touch in virtual environments. These devices can simulate physical sensations when interacting with virtual objects, such as vibrations or resistance.

5. **Object Manipulation:** In some MR scenarios, users may interact with physical objects that are augmented with digital information. For example, a physical book can be enhanced with digital animations or additional information when viewed through an MR headset.

6. **Physics Simulation:** Physics engines are used to simulate the behavior of virtual objects in response to real-world interactions. This includes realistic object collisions, gravity, and forces, making virtual objects behave as if they were physical.

Implementing Physical and Virtual Interactions

Unity Example:

In Unity, you can implement physical and virtual interactions using the AR Foundation package and input handling. Here's a simple example of how you can detect a tap gesture to interact with virtual objects in an AR environment:

using UnityEngine;

using UnityEngine.XR.ARFoundation;

```csharp
using UnityEngine.XR.ARSubsystems;

public class VirtualInteraction : MonoBehaviour

{

private ARRaycastManager raycastManager;

private List<ARRaycastHit> hits = new List<ARRaycastHit>();

private void Awake()

{

raycastManager = GetComponent<ARRaycastManager>();

}

private void Update()

{

if (Input.touchCount > 0)

{

Touch touch = Input.GetTouch(0);

if (touch.phase == TouchPhase.Began)

{

if          (raycastManager.Raycast(touch.position,          hits,
TrackableType.Planes))

{

// A raycast hit a plane, now you can place or interact with virtual
objects at the hit point.
```

```csharp
Vector3 hitPoint = hits[0].pose.position;

PlaceVirtualObject(hitPoint);

}

}

}

}

private void PlaceVirtualObject(Vector3 position)

{

// Implement your logic for placing virtual objects at the specified
position.

}

}
```

This script uses the AR Foundation's ARRaycastManager to perform raycasting against detected planes in the AR environment. When the user taps on a plane, the PlaceVirtualObject function is called, allowing you to instantiate and interact with virtual objects at the hit point.

In summary, physical and virtual interactions are fundamental to creating engaging MR experiences. Leveraging spatial tracking, gestures, voice commands, haptic feedback, and physics simulation, developers can craft immersive mixed reality scenarios that respond seamlessly to user actions, providing a rich and interactive user experience.

Chapter 13: Optical and Visual Effects

Section 13.1: Understanding Human Visual System

Understanding the human visual system is crucial in graphics technology, as it provides insights into how humans perceive visual information. This knowledge helps developers create more immersive and realistic visual effects in various applications, including gaming, simulation, and entertainment.

Basics of Human Vision

The human visual system is complex and remarkable, with several key components:

1. **Eyes:** The eyes capture light and convert it into electrical signals that the brain can interpret. Each eye has a lens that focuses light onto the retina.
2. **Retina:** The retina is a layer of light-sensitive cells at the back of the eye. It contains photoreceptor cells called rods and cones, which are responsible for detecting light and color, respectively.
3. **Optic Nerve:** The optic nerve transmits visual information from the retina to the brain. This information is sent as electrical impulses.
4. **Visual Cortex:** In the brain, the visual cortex processes and interprets the electrical signals received from the optic nerve. It plays a critical role in visual perception.

Visual Perception Principles

To create convincing visual effects, developers need to consider several principles related to human visual perception:

1. **Visual Acuity:** Visual acuity refers to the ability to see fine details. The human eye has higher acuity in the central area of the retina called the fovea. Developers should focus on rendering high-detail content in this area for a more realistic experience.
2. **Color Perception:** Humans perceive a broad spectrum of colors. To create realistic graphics, developers must consider color accuracy, contrast, and the effects of lighting on color perception.
3. **Contrast Sensitivity:** Contrast sensitivity is the ability to distinguish between light and dark areas in an image. Understanding this aspect of vision helps in designing visually appealing scenes with proper lighting and shading.
4. **Motion Perception:** Humans are sensitive to motion. Developers can use motion blur and animation techniques to simulate realistic motion and create a sense of speed or movement.
5. **Depth Perception:** Depth perception allows humans to perceive the relative distance of objects in a scene. Techniques like stereoscopy and depth cues are used in graphics to enhance depth perception.

Simulating Optical Effects

In graphics, simulating optical effects is essential for creating realistic visuals. Some common optical effects include:

- **Bloom:** Bloom simulates the effect of bright light sources by adding a soft, glowing halo around them.

- **Lens Flare:** Lens flare replicates the scattering of light within a camera lens, often seen as bright streaks or spots in images.

- **Chromatic Aberration:** Chromatic aberration mimics the dispersion of light into its constituent colors, creating color fringes around objects.

- **HDR (High Dynamic Range):** HDR techniques capture a broader range of brightness levels in a scene, resulting in more realistic and vibrant visuals.

Understanding human vision and simulating optical effects are vital aspects of graphics technology. By incorporating these principles into their work, developers can create visually stunning and immersive experiences that captivate and engage users.

Section 13.2: Optical Illusions in Graphics

Optical illusions are fascinating phenomena that exploit the quirks of human visual perception. In graphics, designers and developers often use optical illusions intentionally to create compelling and surprising visual effects. Understanding these illusions can be valuable for both artists and engineers working in the field of computer graphics.

Types of Optical Illusions

1. Geometric Illusions:

- *Müller-Lyer Illusion:* This illusion involves two lines of the same length, but one appears longer due to the addition of arrowheads at the ends.

- *Kanizsa Triangle:* Three "Pac-Man" shapes create the illusion of a white triangle in the center.

- *Ponzo Illusion:* Parallel lines appear to converge when placed within converging lines, creating a depth illusion.

2. Color Illusions:

- *Color Afterimage:* Staring at a colored image for an extended time and then looking at a white surface can create an afterimage of complementary colors.

- *Simultaneous Contrast:* The perceived color of an object can change when placed against different-colored backgrounds.

3. Motion Illusions:

- *Rotating Snake Illusion:* Stationary images of snakes appear to rotate when viewed.

- *Phi Phenomenon:* Rapidly displaying images in sequence can create the illusion of continuous motion, as seen in animation.

4. Depth and 3D Illusions:

- *Necker Cube:* A wireframe cube can appear to flip between two 3D orientations.

- *Zöllner Illusion:* Parallel lines appear to be misaligned when crossed by diagonal lines.

Utilizing Optical Illusions in Graphics

Designers and developers can harness optical illusions to enhance user experiences in various ways:

- **Perceived Depth:** Creating illusions of depth in 2D graphics by using shading, perspective, and size relationships.

- **Focus and Attention:** Guiding users' attention to specific elements in a scene using techniques like contrast and color.

- **Visual Comfort:** Avoiding the unintentional creation of discomforting illusions that may strain the viewer's eyes or cause disorientation.

- **Artistic Expression:** Employing optical illusions for artistic purposes, such as creating visually striking and thought-provoking images.

- **Enhancing Realism:** Using illusions to mimic real-world lighting and atmospheric effects, making scenes appear more lifelike.

- **User Interface Design:** Applying illusions to improve the usability and aesthetics of user interfaces in applications and games.

Challenges and Considerations

While optical illusions can be powerful tools in graphics, they come with challenges:

- **Viewer Variability:** Not all viewers perceive illusions in the same way, which can complicate design decisions.

- **Ethical Concerns:** Designers must be mindful of the potential for discomfort or distress caused by certain illusions.

- **Performance Impact:** Complex illusions can be computationally intensive, so developers must balance visual quality with performance.

In conclusion, optical illusions are a captivating aspect of graphics technology. Whether used for artistic expression, enhancing user experiences, or mimicking real-world phenomena, understanding and applying these illusions can lead to visually engaging and memorable graphics.

Section 13.3: Physiological Effects in Graphics

The field of computer graphics extends beyond visual artistry and technical prowess; it also delves into understanding the physiological effects that graphics can have on viewers. Graphics technology has evolved to the point where it can directly impact the human physiological response. In this section, we'll explore some of the physiological effects that graphics can induce and their implications.

HDR and Brightness

High Dynamic Range (HDR) rendering has become commonplace in modern graphics. It enables the display of a wider range of brightness levels, from deep blacks to intense whites. While HDR can enhance visual realism, it also poses physiological challenges. Excessive brightness can lead to discomfort, glare, and even visual fatigue. Developers must carefully balance HDR effects to ensure they enhance rather than detract from the user experience.

Color and Emotional Response

Colors in graphics can evoke strong emotional responses. For example, warm colors like red and orange can convey excitement and intensity, while cool colors like blue and green can create a sense of calm. Understanding color psychology is crucial in design to convey the intended emotional tone of a scene or user interface. However, individual differences in color perception mean that designers must consider a wide range of viewers' responses.

Flicker and Motion Sickness

Flickering graphics, especially at certain frequencies, can induce discomfort and even motion sickness in some viewers. This phenomenon is more prevalent in virtual reality (VR) and augmented reality (AR) environments, where head-mounted displays introduce new challenges. Developers must minimize flicker and optimize frame rates to ensure a comfortable experience, particularly in immersive VR settings.

Accessibility Considerations

Physiological diversity among users demands careful consideration of accessibility. Designers and developers must accommodate individuals with photosensitive epilepsy or other visual sensitivities. This includes avoiding rapidly flashing lights or high-contrast patterns that could trigger adverse reactions.

Ergonomics and Prolonged Use

Graphics that demand prolonged viewing, such as video games or extended VR experiences, can strain users' eyes and lead to discomfort or fatigue. Ergonomics, including proper lighting, display positioning, and break reminders, play a crucial role in reducing these physiological effects.

Ethical Implications

The potential to influence human physiology through graphics also raises ethical questions. Developers must be mindful of creating content that respects viewers' well-being. This includes avoiding content that may induce distress, discomfort, or addiction-like behaviors.

In conclusion, the impact of graphics on human physiology is a multidimensional consideration in the field of computer graphics. Designers and developers must be attuned to the physiological effects of their creations, striving to enhance user experiences while ensuring comfort, safety, and accessibility for all viewers. This understanding can lead to more responsible and effective graphics development practices.

Section 13.4: Adaptive Rendering Techniques

Adaptive rendering techniques are a significant advancement in the field of computer graphics. They offer the capability to dynamically adjust rendering parameters and quality settings in response to various factors, including system performance, user preferences, and the context of the application. In this section, we'll explore the concept of adaptive rendering and its practical applications.

Dynamic Quality Adjustment

One of the primary objectives of adaptive rendering is to maintain a consistent frame rate while optimizing visual quality. When a graphics application detects that the system is struggling to maintain a target frame rate, it can dynamically reduce the quality of rendering. This may involve lowering texture resolutions, simplifying geometry, or reducing the number of visual effects. Conversely, when the system has ample resources, the rendering quality can be increased to enhance visual fidelity.

User-Defined Preferences

Adaptive rendering allows users to customize their graphics experience. This includes options to adjust settings such as texture quality, shadow complexity, and anti-aliasing levels. These user-defined preferences provide a more personalized experience and cater to a wide range of hardware capabilities.

Context-Aware Rendering

Context-aware rendering takes into account the specific context in which a graphics application is being used. For example, in a virtual reality (VR) application, the adaptive rendering system might prioritize rendering quality for objects in the user's immediate field of view while reducing detail for objects in the periphery. This not only improves performance but also enhances the sense of immersion.

Runtime Performance Metrics

Adaptive rendering relies on real-time performance metrics to make informed decisions. These metrics can include frame rate, GPU and CPU load, memory usage, and even the temperature of system components. By continuously monitoring these metrics, the application can make instant adjustments to maintain optimal performance.

Challenges and Trade-offs

While adaptive rendering offers numerous benefits, it also presents challenges. Implementing adaptive systems can be complex, requiring careful consideration of how to adjust rendering parameters without causing visual artifacts or abrupt changes in quality. Striking the right balance between performance and visual quality is an ongoing process.

Future Directions

As hardware capabilities continue to evolve, adaptive rendering techniques will play an increasingly vital role in graphics development. Artificial intelligence and machine learning can further enhance adaptive systems by predicting user preferences and system performance, making real-time adjustments even more seamless.

In conclusion, adaptive rendering techniques represent a significant step forward in the field of computer graphics. They enable applications to provide tailored, high-quality experiences across a wide range of hardware while responding to changing conditions and user preferences. As technology continues to advance, adaptive rendering will remain a key area of innovation in graphics development.

Section 13.5: Future of Display Technologies

The future of display technologies is a topic of great excitement and anticipation in the field of computer graphics. Advancements in displays have a direct impact on how we experience digital content, from video games to virtual reality (VR) environments. In this section, we'll explore some of the key trends and developments expected to shape the future of display technologies.

1. Higher Resolution Displays

One of the most immediate trends is the continuous push for higher display resolutions. From 4K to 8K and beyond, increased pixel density results in sharper and more detailed visuals. This trend benefits various applications, including gaming, professional content creation, and medical imaging.

2. Refresh Rate Innovations

Higher refresh rates are becoming standard, especially in gaming monitors. Displays with 120Hz, 144Hz, or even 240Hz refresh rates offer smoother motion and reduced motion blur. This is crucial for fast-paced gaming experiences and VR applications where motion sickness can be a concern.

3. HDR (High Dynamic Range)

HDR technology enhances the contrast and color accuracy of displays. It allows for a wider range of brightness levels, resulting in more lifelike and vibrant visuals. As HDR content becomes more prevalent, displays that support this technology are in high demand.

4. OLED and MicroLED Displays

Organic Light Emitting Diode (OLED) and MicroLED displays are gaining popularity due to their ability to offer deep blacks, high contrast ratios, and thinner form factors. OLED is commonly used in smartphones, while MicroLED holds promise for larger displays and VR headsets.

5. Flexible and Foldable Displays

Flexible and foldable displays are opening up new possibilities for device form factors. Devices like foldable smartphones and tablets offer compactness and versatility, and these technologies could extend to larger displays in the future.

6. Augmented Reality (AR) and Mixed Reality (MR)

AR and MR technologies rely heavily on innovative displays. AR glasses aim to blend digital and physical worlds seamlessly, providing real-time information and interactive experiences. The development of lightweight and immersive AR glasses is a significant focus for display manufacturers.

7. Holographic Displays

Holographic displays are a futuristic concept that aims to create three-dimensional, interactive holograms. While still in the experimental stages, progress is being made in this area, and it holds potential for applications in entertainment, education, and design.

8. Biometric Displays

Displays are increasingly integrating biometric sensors, such as fingerprint scanners and facial recognition cameras. These features enhance security and enable personalized user experiences.

9. Energy-Efficient Displays

Efforts are being made to develop displays that consume less power, which is crucial for extending battery life in portable devices and reducing energy consumption in larger displays.

10. Sustainability

Sustainability is a growing concern in display technology. Manufacturers are exploring eco-friendly materials and manufacturing processes to reduce the environmental impact of displays.

In summary, the future of display technologies holds tremendous potential to transform how we interact with digital content. From higher resolutions and refresh rates to innovative form factors and technologies like AR and holography, the evolution of displays promises exciting possibilities for the fields of entertainment, education, healthcare, and beyond. As these technologies continue to advance, they will shape the way we perceive and engage with the digital world.

Chapter 14: Advanced Networking and Cloud Integration

In this chapter, we dive into the world of advanced networking and cloud integration in the context of computer graphics. Networking and cloud technologies play a crucial role in modern graphics applications, enabling features such as multiplayer gaming, cloud-rendered graphics, and real-time collaboration. We will explore various aspects of this domain, from optimizing network communication in games to leveraging the cloud for graphics processing.

Section 14.1: Cloud-rendered Graphics

Cloud-rendered graphics, often referred to as cloud gaming or game streaming, represent a paradigm shift in how games are delivered and played. With cloud-rendered graphics, the heavy lifting of rendering complex 3D scenes is shifted from the player's device to remote servers in data centers. Players receive video streams of the game, and their input commands are sent to the cloud for processing. This approach has several advantages and challenges:

Advantages:

1. **Accessibility:** Cloud-rendered games can be played on a wide range of devices, including smartphones, tablets, smart TVs, and low-end PCs, as the rendering workload is handled remotely.
2. **High-Quality Graphics:** Games can be played at the highest graphical settings, even on devices that wouldn't typically support such graphics locally.
3. **Instant Play:** There's no need for lengthy downloads or installations. Players can start playing almost instantly.
4. **Cross-Platform Play:** Cloud gaming platforms often support cross-platform play, allowing players on different devices to play together.

Challenges:

1. **Latency:** The most significant challenge in cloud-rendered graphics is latency. Since player inputs must be sent to the cloud data center and the video stream returned, even a slight delay can impact gameplay. Minimizing latency is a top priority for cloud gaming providers.
2. **Bandwidth:** Streaming high-quality video and audio

requires substantial bandwidth. Players with slow or limited internet connections may have a suboptimal experience.

3. **Data Centers:** Cloud gaming depends on the availability and proximity of data centers. Players far from data centers may experience higher latency.

4. **Ownership and Licensing:** Cloud gaming raises questions about game ownership and licensing, as players may not have physical copies of games.

Implementation:

Implementing cloud-rendered graphics involves setting up a data center infrastructure capable of rendering games in real-time and streaming them to players. This requires powerful GPUs, low-latency networking, and specialized software for video encoding and decoding. Popular cloud gaming platforms include Google Stadia, NVIDIA GeForce NOW, and Microsoft's Xbox Cloud Gaming.

In conclusion, cloud-rendered graphics represent a disruptive technology in the world of gaming and graphics applications. While they offer accessibility and high-quality visuals, addressing challenges like latency and bandwidth is critical for widespread adoption. As technology continues to improve, cloud-rendered graphics have the potential to revolutionize how we experience interactive 3D content.

Section 14.2: Real-time Stream Decomposition

Real-time stream decomposition is a crucial technique in advanced networking for graphics applications. It involves breaking down complex data streams into manageable parts for efficient transmission, processing, and rendering. This technique is particularly relevant in scenarios where large and complex graphics or multimedia data must be transmitted over a network or processed in real-time. In this section, we will explore the concept of real-time stream decomposition, its importance, and some implementation considerations.

The Importance of Stream Decomposition

Graphics and multimedia data, such as video, audio, or 3D models, can be extremely data-intensive. Transmitting or processing such data in its raw form can be inefficient and may lead to issues like high latency, network congestion, or slow rendering performance. Real-time stream decomposition addresses these challenges by dividing data streams into smaller, more manageable units, often referred to as "packets" or "chunks."

Advantages of Stream Decomposition:

1. **Reduced Latency:** By breaking down data into smaller units, the latency associated with transmitting or processing large files can be minimized. Smaller packets can be processed more quickly.
2. **Efficient Bandwidth Usage:** Decomposing streams allows for better bandwidth utilization. Only the required portions of data are transmitted or processed, reducing unnecessary overhead.
3. **Robustness:** In networked applications, such as online gaming or video streaming, stream decomposition can enhance robustness. If one packet is lost or corrupted during transmission, it affects only a portion of the data, minimizing the impact on the overall experience.

Implementing Real-time Stream Decomposition

The implementation of real-time stream decomposition depends on the nature of the data and the specific requirements of the application. Here are some key considerations:

1. **Packetization:** Data streams are divided into packets or chunks. The size of these packets can vary depending on the application and network conditions. Smaller packets reduce latency but may increase overhead.

2. **Header Information:** Each packet typically includes header information that describes the packet's content and how it fits into the larger stream. This header information is essential for proper reconstruction on the receiving end.

3. **Synchronization:** In multimedia applications, synchronization between different streams (e.g., audio and video) is critical. Properly timestamping and synchronizing packets ensures that audio and video stay aligned.

4. **Error Handling:** Robust error handling mechanisms are crucial. Lost or corrupted packets should be detected and, if possible, recovered or compensated for to maintain data integrity.

5. **Buffering:** On the receiving end, buffers are used to store incoming packets temporarily before they are processed or rendered. Buffering helps smooth out variations in packet arrival times.

6. **Quality of Service (QoS):** Depending on the application's requirements, QoS mechanisms may be employed to prioritize the delivery of certain packets, ensuring that critical data is transmitted with minimal delay.

In conclusion, real-time stream decomposition is a fundamental technique in networking for graphics and multimedia applications.

It enables efficient transmission and processing of large and complex data streams while minimizing latency and improving the overall user experience. Implementing stream decomposition involves careful consideration of packetization, synchronization, error handling, buffering, and QoS to meet the specific needs of the application.

Section 14.3: Multiplayer VR and AR Systems

Multiplayer Virtual Reality (VR) and Augmented Reality (AR) systems represent a significant advancement in immersive technology. These systems enable users to interact with each other in shared virtual or augmented spaces, creating collaborative and social experiences. In this section, we will delve into the concepts, challenges, and technologies behind multiplayer VR and AR systems.

The Essence of Multiplayer Immersion

Multiplayer VR and AR systems aim to bring people together in shared digital environments, whether they are physically distant or in the same physical space. These systems combine the power of VR or AR headsets with network connectivity to enable users to see, hear, and interact with each other as digital avatars or holograms. This fusion of technologies offers several advantages:

1. **Social Interaction:** Multiplayer VR and AR enhance social experiences. Users can see and interact with friends, colleagues, or strangers as if they were in the same room, regardless of their physical locations.

2. **Collaboration:** These systems enable collaborative work, training, or gaming. Multiple users can work together on projects, simulate scenarios, or play games that require

teamwork.

3. **Presence:** The feeling of "presence" is crucial. Users feel as if they are physically present in the digital environment, thanks to the immersive qualities of VR and AR.

4. **Shared Experiences:** Users can share experiences, such as attending virtual events, exploring educational simulations, or visiting virtual museums, adding a new dimension to entertainment and learning.

Challenges in Multiplayer VR and AR

Building multiplayer VR and AR systems comes with unique challenges:

1. **Latency:** Minimizing latency is crucial to maintain the feeling of presence. Even slight delays in tracking or interactions can disrupt the immersive experience.

2. **Network Congestion:** High-quality VR and AR experiences demand substantial bandwidth. Network congestion can lead to packet loss and degraded experiences.

3. **Synchronization:** Ensuring that all users experience the same events at the same time is challenging. Achieving perfect synchronization is often impossible due to network variability.

4. **Content Creation:** Creating compelling content for multiplayer VR and AR requires specialized skills in 3D modeling, animation, and user interface design.

5. **Privacy and Security:** Protecting user data and ensuring secure interactions is a paramount concern in multiplayer environments.

Technologies in Multiplayer VR and AR

Several technologies underpin multiplayer VR and AR systems:

1. **Networking Protocols:** Real-time communication relies on protocols like WebRTC and custom solutions for low-latency data exchange.
2. **Cloud Computing:** Cloud-based services are used for hosting and managing shared experiences, offloading computational tasks, and storing user data.
3. **Positional Tracking:** Precise tracking of user movements is essential for maintaining immersion. Systems use sensors, cameras, or external tracking systems.
4. **Content Delivery:** High-quality 3D models, textures, and audio are delivered on-demand or streamed from servers to maintain visual and auditory fidelity.
5. **Social Integration:** Integration with social media and communication platforms enhances social interactions within the VR or AR environment.
6. **Security Measures:** Encryption, authentication, and access control are implemented to protect user data and ensure safe interactions.

In conclusion, multiplayer VR and AR systems have the potential to revolutionize how people interact, collaborate, and engage in immersive experiences. While they offer numerous benefits, they also present challenges related to latency, synchronization, content creation, and security. Advancements in networking, cloud computing, tracking, and content delivery are continuously driving the evolution of multiplayer VR and AR, making these technologies increasingly accessible and compelling.

Section 14.4: Server-side Physics and Logic

Server-side physics and logic play a pivotal role in multiplayer online games and virtual worlds. These components ensure consistent and fair interactions among players while offloading complex calculations from individual client devices. In this section, we explore the significance of server-side physics and logic and how they contribute to the multiplayer gaming experience.

The Role of Server-side Physics

Physics simulations are integral to many games, especially those involving real-world physics, such as collision detection, object dynamics, and gravity. In single-player games, these simulations are typically executed on the player's device (client-side). However, in multiplayer scenarios, relying solely on client-side physics can lead to inconsistencies, cheating, and synchronization issues.

Server-side physics involve performing physics calculations on a centralized server, which acts as an authoritative source of truth. Key aspects of server-side physics include:

1. **Consistency:** By performing physics calculations on the server, all players receive consistent results. This ensures that interactions, such as collisions or object movements, are identical for every player in the game.

2. **Cheating Prevention:** Server-side physics makes it more challenging for players to manipulate the game by altering client-side physics calculations. Cheating prevention mechanisms are enforced on the server.

3. **Bandwidth Optimization:** Transmitting the results of physics simulations (e.g., object positions) instead of the physics calculations themselves reduces the amount of data sent over the network, optimizing bandwidth.

Implementing Server-side Logic

Server-side logic extends beyond physics and encompasses game rules, objectives, and interactions. It ensures that the game's state is consistent across all clients and that actions taken by one player affect the entire game world consistently.

Key components of server-side logic include:

1. **Game State Management:** The server maintains the authoritative game state, including player positions, scores, and object statuses. Clients query the server to obtain this information.
2. **Player Interactions:** Server-side logic handles player actions, such as shooting, item pickups, and character abilities, ensuring fair and consistent outcomes for all players.
3. **Event Handling:** Events like player deaths, level transitions, or game-over conditions are managed by the server, which communicates these events to all clients.
4. **Anti-Cheating Measures:** Server-side logic implements anti-cheating mechanisms to detect and prevent unauthorized actions or manipulations of the game state.

Challenges and Considerations

Implementing server-side physics and logic is not without challenges:

1. **Latency:** Server-side calculations introduce additional latency compared to client-side physics. Minimizing this latency is crucial to maintain a responsive gaming experience.
2. **Scalability:** Online multiplayer games must accommodate

a varying number of players. Scalability is essential to ensure that the server can handle increased loads.

3. **Synchronization:** Achieving perfect synchronization is challenging due to network latency and variations. Developers often employ techniques like interpolation and prediction to mitigate synchronization issues.

4. **Security:** Ensuring the security of server-side logic is critical to prevent cheating, unauthorized access, and data breaches.

In conclusion, server-side physics and logic are vital components of multiplayer online games and virtual worlds. They provide consistency, fairness, and security while enabling complex interactions and simulations that enhance the gaming experience. Implementing these components requires careful consideration of latency, scalability, synchronization, and security to deliver engaging and cheat-free multiplayer experiences.

Section 14.5: Scalable Game Servers and Microservices

Scalability is a crucial consideration in modern multiplayer games, particularly in the context of large-scale online games with massive player bases. In this section, we explore the concept of scalable game servers and how microservices architecture can be leveraged to achieve it.

The Need for Scalability

As a multiplayer game gains popularity, it attracts more players, resulting in increased server loads and demands on the backend infrastructure. To maintain a smooth gaming experience and accommodate a growing player base, game developers must design their server architecture to be scalable.

Scalability in this context refers to the ability to handle more players and game instances without a significant drop in performance. The traditional approach of running monolithic game servers on dedicated hardware may become a bottleneck as the player base grows.

Microservices Architecture

Microservices architecture is an architectural style that breaks down a monolithic application into a collection of smaller, independently deployable services. Each service is responsible for a specific aspect of the application's functionality. When applied to multiplayer games, microservices can help achieve scalability in several ways:

1. **Load Distribution:** Microservices can be deployed across multiple servers or cloud instances. This distribution helps distribute the load more evenly, preventing a single server from becoming a performance bottleneck.
2. **Independent Scaling:** Each microservice can be scaled independently based on its resource requirements. For example, services handling player authentication or chat functionality can be scaled differently from those managing game instances.
3. **Fault Isolation:** Isolating different game features into microservices allows for fault isolation. If one service experiences issues, it won't necessarily affect the entire game, reducing downtime and improving fault tolerance.

Components of Scalable Game Servers

To implement scalable game servers using microservices, consider
the following components:

1. **Game Instances:** Each game instance, such as a match or
   level, can be considered a microservice. These instances are
   created dynamically to accommodate new players and can
   be distributed across servers as needed.
2. **Player Services:** Services for player authentication,
   matchmaking, and player profiles can be implemented as
   microservices. These services can scale independently to
   handle registration spikes and ensure smooth
   matchmaking.
3. **Game Logic Services:** The core game logic, including
   rules, physics, and interactions, can be divided into
   separate microservices. This allows for flexible scaling and
   easier updates to specific game mechanics.
4. **Communication Middleware:** Implement messaging and
   communication services that allow microservices to
   communicate efficiently. Message queues, publish-
   subscribe systems, and WebSocket-based solutions can
   facilitate real-time interactions.
5. **Monitoring and Autoscaling:** Utilize monitoring tools
   and autoscaling mechanisms to automatically adjust the
   number of microservice instances based on resource
   utilization and player demand.

Challenges and Considerations

Scalable game servers and microservices introduce challenges such
as:

1. **Complexity:** Managing a microservices architecture can

be more complex than a monolithic server. Tools for orchestration, monitoring, and debugging become essential.

2. **Data Consistency:** Maintaining data consistency across distributed microservices requires careful design and the use of distributed databases or data synchronization techniques.

3. **Latency:** Introducing microservices can add latency due to inter-service communication. Optimization is needed to keep communication efficient.

4. **Security:** Microservices should be secured individually and collectively to prevent unauthorized access or data breaches.

In summary, scalable game servers and microservices architecture are critical for accommodating large player bases in modern multiplayer games. This approach offers flexibility, load distribution, and fault tolerance. However, it also introduces complexity and requires careful planning, monitoring, and security measures to ensure a responsive and secure gaming experience.

Chapter 15: Security and Anti-cheat Mechanisms

Section 15.1: Understanding Common Exploits

Security in computer graphics applications is crucial to prevent various exploits and vulnerabilities that can potentially harm users, compromise data, or disrupt gameplay experiences. Understanding common exploits is the first step in creating a robust security strategy for your graphics software.

The Importance of Security

Security vulnerabilities in graphics applications can have severe consequences. Exploits can lead to unauthorized access, data breaches, cheating in multiplayer games, and more. Therefore, it's essential to be proactive in identifying and mitigating potential risks.

Common Graphics Exploits

1. **Buffer Overflows**: Buffer overflows occur when data is written beyond the boundaries of a buffer, leading to memory corruption. In graphics applications, buffer overflows can be used to execute arbitrary code or crash the application.
2. **Shader Injection**: Attackers can inject malicious code into shaders, which are widely used in graphics programming. This can lead to graphics card crashes, application instability, or even unauthorized access to system resources.
3. **Texture Manipulation**: Texture manipulation exploits involve tampering with textures used in a game or

application. Attackers can modify textures to gain an unfair advantage in multiplayer games or to display inappropriate content.

4. **Rendering Attacks**: Graphics rendering attacks exploit vulnerabilities in the rendering pipeline. For example, attackers may use shader programs to hide objects or render objects incorrectly.

5. **Anti-aliasing Manipulation**: Anti-aliasing is a common technique used to improve graphics quality. Attackers may manipulate anti-aliasing settings to gain an advantage or disrupt the user's experience.

6. **Resource Exhaustion**: By consuming excessive GPU or CPU resources, attackers can cause the application to slow down or become unresponsive, leading to a poor user experience.

Mitigation Strategies

To protect against these exploits, consider the following mitigation strategies:

- **Input Validation**: Always validate user inputs to prevent buffer overflows and injection attacks.

- **Shader Sanitization**: Carefully review and sanitize shader code to prevent injection attacks.

- **Texture Verification**: Implement checks to ensure the integrity of textures and prevent tampering.

- **Rendering Pipeline Security**: Secure the rendering pipeline to prevent rendering attacks.

- **Resource Management**: Implement resource management strategies to prevent resource exhaustion.

- **Regular Updates**: Keep your graphics software up-to-date to patch known vulnerabilities.

- **Anti-cheat Mechanisms**: In multiplayer games, implement anti-cheat mechanisms to detect and prevent cheating.

By understanding common exploits and implementing security measures, you can create graphics applications that are not only visually impressive but also secure for users.

Section 15.2: Secure OpenGL Programming

Secure OpenGL programming is essential to prevent potential security vulnerabilities and ensure the safety of your graphics applications. OpenGL, a widely used graphics API, offers various features and capabilities, but it's crucial to use them securely to protect against common exploits. In this section, we'll explore best practices for secure OpenGL programming.

Use Shader Validation

Shaders are a fundamental part of OpenGL programming, and they are often written in OpenGL Shader Language (GLSL). It's essential to validate shader code to prevent shader injection attacks. Shader code should be sanitized and reviewed thoroughly to ensure it doesn't contain any malicious instructions.

// Shader validation example in OpenGL

```
GLuint vertexShader = glCreateShader(GL_VERTEX_SHADER);

glShaderSource(vertexShader, 1, &vertexShaderSource, NULL);

glCompileShader(vertexShader);

// Check for shader compilation errors

int success;

char infoLog[512];

glGetShaderiv(vertexShader, GL_COMPILE_STATUS, &success);

if (!success) {

glGetShaderInfoLog(vertexShader, 512, NULL, infoLog);

fprintf(stderr, "Vertex shader compilation failed: %s\n", infoLog);

}
```

Validate Input Data

OpenGL applications often receive input data from users or external sources. It's critical to validate and sanitize this data to prevent buffer overflows and other security issues. Ensure that data passed to OpenGL functions doesn't exceed buffer boundaries.

```
// Input data validation example

if (dataSize > bufferSize) {

fprintf(stderr, "Data size exceeds buffer size. Aborting.\n");

exit(EXIT_FAILURE);
```

```
}
```

Properly Manage OpenGL Resources

Managing OpenGL resources like textures, buffers, and shaders is essential for both performance and security. Improper resource management can lead to resource exhaustion exploits. Always release resources when they are no longer needed to free up GPU memory and other system resources.

```
// Properly deleting OpenGL resources

glDeleteShader(shader);

glDeleteTextures(1, &texture);

glDeleteBuffers(1, &vbo);
```

Enable OpenGL Debugging

Modern OpenGL implementations often include debugging features that can help identify potential issues in your code. Enabling OpenGL debugging can provide valuable insights into problems like rendering attacks or incorrect usage of OpenGL functions.

```
// Enable OpenGL debugging

glEnable(GL_DEBUG_OUTPUT);

glDebugMessageCallback(DebugCallback, NULL);

// Debug callback function

void APIENTRY DebugCallback(GLenum source, GLenum type, GLuint id, GLenum severity, GLsizei length, const GLchar* message, const void* userParam) {
```

```
fprintf(stderr, "OpenGL Debug Message: %s\n", message);

}
```

Keep OpenGL Libraries and Drivers Updated

Graphics libraries and GPU drivers should be kept up-to-date to take advantage of security patches and bug fixes. Outdated libraries or drivers may contain known vulnerabilities that attackers can exploit.

Secure OpenGL programming is a crucial aspect of creating graphics applications that not only provide great visual experiences but also protect users from potential security threats. By following these best practices and staying vigilant for potential security issues, you can enhance the security of your OpenGL applications.

Section 15.3: Anti-cheat Techniques and Mechanisms

Ensuring fair play and preventing cheating in online games is a significant concern for game developers and players alike. Cheating not only ruins the gaming experience but can also lead to economic losses for developers and publishers. In this section, we'll explore anti-cheat techniques and mechanisms that game developers can employ to combat cheating.

1. Server-Side Verification

One of the fundamental anti-cheat measures is to perform critical game logic and verification on the server-side. By relying on server-side validation, you can ensure that all game actions and events are consistent with the game rules and prevent clients from manipulating game data.

```python
# Server-side verification example (Python)

def handle_player_movement(player_id, new_position):

    # Retrieve player data from the server

    player_data = get_player_data(player_id)

    # Check if the movement is valid based on server data

    if is_valid_movement(player_data, new_position):

        # Update player position on the server

        update_player_position(player_id, new_position)

    else:

        # Notify the client of an invalid movement

        notify_invalid_movement(player_id)
```

2. Encrypted Communication

Using encrypted communication protocols between the client and server can prevent data tampering and eavesdropping. Encryption ensures that game-related information remains confidential and maintains the integrity of the data exchanged between the client and server.

3. Anti-cheat Software

Integrate third-party anti-cheat software into your game. Companies like BattlEye and Easy Anti-Cheat provide solutions that can detect and prevent various cheating methods, such as aimbots, wallhacks, and speed hacks.

4. Behavioral Analysis

Implement behavioral analysis algorithms to detect unusual or suspicious player behavior. This can include tracking player movement patterns, aiming accuracy, and other in-game actions. Deviations from normal behavior can trigger investigations or penalties.

```cpp
// Behavioral analysis example (C++)

void CheckPlayerBehavior(Player player) {

if (IsUnusuallyAccurate(player)) {

// Flag the player for further investigation

FlagPlayerForReview(player);

}

}
```

5. Regular Updates and Patching

Frequent game updates and patches can help in combating cheats. Cheating software often relies on specific game versions and vulnerabilities. By regularly updating the game and addressing security issues, you can render many cheats ineffective.

6. Reporting Systems

Provide players with a mechanism to report suspected cheaters. Investigate these reports and take appropriate actions, such as issuing temporary or permanent bans if cheating is confirmed.

7. Machine Learning

Leverage machine learning models to detect cheating patterns automatically. These models can analyze large datasets of player behavior to identify anomalies and cheats.

 # Machine learning cheat detection (Python)

def detect_cheating_behavior(player_data):

 # Train a machine learning model with historical data

model = train_cheat_detection_model(historical_data)

 # Predict whether the player is cheating

prediction = model.predict(player_data)

if prediction == "cheating":

 # Take appropriate action (e.g., ban the player)

handle_cheater(player_data)

8. Fair Play Policies

Clearly communicate your game's fair play policies to players. Let them know what is considered cheating and what the consequences are. Transparency can discourage cheating and help build a positive gaming community.

9. Continuous Monitoring

Maintain a dedicated team to monitor and respond to cheating reports and emerging cheating techniques. Staying vigilant is essential as cheat developers are constantly evolving their methods.

Preventing cheating in online games is an ongoing challenge, but by implementing a combination of these anti-cheat techniques and mechanisms, game developers can create a more fair and enjoyable gaming experience for all players.

Section 15.4: Encrypted Networking in Games

In the world of online gaming, secure and encrypted networking is crucial to protect players' data, maintain game integrity, and prevent cheating. This section explores the importance of encrypted networking in games and how it can be implemented.

1. Why Encrypted Networking?

1.1 Data Privacy and Protection

One of the primary reasons for using encrypted networking in games is to protect players' data. This includes login credentials, personal information, and in-game communications. Encryption ensures that even if malicious actors intercept the network traffic, they cannot decipher the sensitive information.

1.2 Game Integrity

To maintain the integrity of the game, it's essential to prevent cheating and tampering with game data. Encrypted networking makes it challenging for cheaters to manipulate game packets and gain an unfair advantage.

2. Implementing Encrypted Networking

2.1 Secure Protocols

Choose secure communication protocols that offer encryption by default. Secure Sockets Layer (SSL) and its successor, Transport Layer Security (TLS), are commonly used protocols for securing network communications in games.

2.2 End-to-End Encryption

Implement end-to-end encryption whenever possible. This means that data is encrypted on the sender's side and only decrypted on the receiver's side. It ensures that even the game server cannot access the contents of messages exchanged between players.

2.3 Public and Private Keys

Encryption often involves the use of public and private keys. Players can generate public-private key pairs during registration, and the public keys can be shared with others for secure communication. Messages encrypted with a player's public key can only be decrypted with their corresponding private key.

2.4 Data Packet Encryption

Encrypt game data packets to protect them from eavesdropping. When players send their actions or movements to the server or other players, these packets should be encrypted to prevent tampering.

// Encrypting a game data packet (Java)

```
byte[] encryptedPacket = encryptGameData(playerData,
recipientPublicKey);

sendEncryptedPacket(encryptedPacket);
```

3. Key Management

3.1 Key Rotation

Regularly rotate encryption keys to enhance security. Key rotation helps mitigate the risk of a compromised key being used for an extended period. Implementing key rotation can be a complex but necessary process.

3.2 Key Exchange

Use secure methods for exchanging encryption keys, especially in multiplayer games. Key exchange protocols like the Diffie-Hellman key exchange allow players to securely share encryption keys without exposing them to potential attackers.

4. Encryption Overhead

It's important to note that encryption introduces some computational overhead. Encrypting and decrypting data can consume additional CPU resources, so game developers should strike a balance between security and performance.

5. Regulatory Compliance

In some regions, there are legal requirements for protecting user data, including encryption standards. Game developers must be aware of and compliant with these regulations, such as the General Data Protection Regulation (GDPR) in Europe.

6. Conclusion

Encrypted networking is a critical component of modern online gaming. It safeguards player data, maintains game integrity, and helps prevent cheating. While implementing encryption adds complexity, it is a necessary step to ensure a secure and enjoyable gaming experience for players worldwide.

Section 15.5: Forensics and Post-breach Analysis

In the world of online gaming, maintaining security is an ongoing battle. Despite robust security measures, breaches can occur, and it's crucial to be prepared for post-breach analysis and forensics to understand what happened and prevent future incidents. This section delves into the world of forensics and post-breach analysis in the context of gaming security.

1. The Importance of Post-Breach Analysis

1.1 Learning from Incidents

When a security breach occurs in an online game, it's essential to treat it as an opportunity to learn and improve. Post-breach analysis helps identify vulnerabilities and weaknesses in the security infrastructure.

1.2 Preventing Recurrence

Understanding the nature of the breach and the attacker's tactics allows game developers to implement countermeasures to prevent similar incidents from happening again.

2. Gathering Evidence

2.1 Log Analysis

Game servers generate extensive logs of player activities. These logs can be invaluable in determining how a breach occurred. Analyzing logs can reveal unusual patterns of behavior or unauthorized access.

2.2 Network Traffic Analysis

Examining network traffic can provide insights into how attackers gained access to the game server or player data. Network packet captures can reveal the methods and tools used by attackers.

2.3 System Memory Analysis

In cases of cheating or tampering, analyzing the memory of the game client or server can help identify malicious code or injected modifications. Memory forensics tools are essential for this task.

3. Collaborating with Law Enforcement

In severe cases of security breaches, it may be necessary to collaborate with law enforcement agencies. This involves providing evidence and cooperating in criminal investigations. Legal and ethical considerations are paramount in these situations.

4. Strengthening Security

4.1 Patching Vulnerabilities

Identified vulnerabilities should be promptly patched to prevent future exploitation. Game developers should maintain a rigorous patching process to address security issues.

4.2 Enhancing Monitoring

Implement advanced monitoring systems that can detect and alert on suspicious activities in real-time. Intrusion detection and prevention systems (IDPS) can be valuable for this purpose.

4.3 Educating the Team

Security awareness and training are essential for all members of the development team. This includes not only developers but also support staff and administrators who handle player data.

5. Public Communication

In the event of a breach, it's essential to communicate transparently with players. Inform them about the breach, what data may have been exposed, and the steps being taken to improve security. Maintaining trust is crucial.

6. Legal and Regulatory Compliance

Ensure that the handling of security breaches aligns with legal and regulatory requirements, especially concerning data protection and privacy laws.

7. Conclusion

In the dynamic world of online gaming, security breaches are a risk that developers must be prepared to face. Post-breach analysis, forensics, and a commitment to continuous improvement are essential components of a comprehensive security strategy. By learning from incidents, strengthening security measures, and collaborating with law enforcement when necessary, game developers can better protect their players and their games.

Chapter 16: Toolchain and Workflow Mastery

In the world of computer graphics and game development, mastering your toolchain and workflow is crucial for efficiency, productivity, and the creation of high-quality graphics and games. This chapter explores various aspects of toolchains and workflows that can help you streamline your development process.

Section 16.1: Advanced Debugging Techniques

Debugging is an integral part of software development, and in the context of graphics programming, it takes on a unique set of challenges. This section delves into advanced debugging techniques tailored to graphics and game development.

1. Debugging Graphics Shaders

1.1 Shader Debugging Tools

Debugging shaders can be challenging due to their parallel nature. Learn about specialized shader debugging tools and techniques that allow you to inspect shader code during runtime.

1.2 GPU Profiling

GPU profiling tools help you identify bottlenecks in your graphics pipeline. Explore various GPU profiling techniques and tools to optimize your rendering performance.

2. Real-time Debugging

2.1 Remote Debugging

Discover how to set up remote debugging sessions for graphics applications, which can be particularly useful when debugging on different platforms or hardware configurations.

2.2 Frame Debugging

Frame debugging techniques allow you to step through the rendering process frame by frame, inspecting render targets and intermediate buffers to identify rendering issues.

3. Memory Debugging

3.1 Memory Leaks and GPU Resources

Graphics applications can suffer from memory leaks and resource management problems. Learn how to use memory debugging tools to detect and fix these issues.

3.2 Memory Analysis for Performance

Optimizing memory usage is critical for performance. Explore memory analysis tools and strategies to minimize memory overhead in your graphics applications.

4. Crash Analysis

4.1 Crash Dump Analysis

When your graphics application crashes, analyzing crash dumps can provide insights into the cause. Learn how to perform effective crash dump analysis to identify and resolve issues.

5. Collaborative Debugging

5.1 Collaborative Debugging Tools

Graphics development often involves collaboration among team members. Discover tools and practices that facilitate collaborative debugging, including version control systems and issue tracking.

6. Advanced Debugging Tips

6.1 Conditional Breakpoints

Conditional breakpoints allow you to break execution only when specific conditions are met, making it easier to pinpoint issues in complex code.

6.2 Visual Debugging

Visual debugging techniques, such as rendering debug overlays or visualizing GPU data, can provide a more intuitive way to identify problems in your graphics application.

7. Post-mortem Analysis

7.1 Post-mortem Analysis Tools

Learn about post-mortem analysis tools that help you analyze and diagnose issues that occurred in production or during user testing.

8. Continuous Integration for Debugging

8.1 Automated Testing and Debugging

Integrate automated testing and debugging into your continuous integration (CI) pipeline to catch issues early in the development process.

9. Conclusion

Mastering advanced debugging techniques tailored to graphics and game development is essential for creating visually stunning and stable graphics applications. With the right tools and strategies, you can streamline the debugging process, identify and resolve issues efficiently, and ultimately deliver a polished gaming experience to your players.

Section 16.2: Continuous Integration for Graphics Projects

Continuous Integration (CI) is a software development practice that focuses on automating the building, testing, and deployment of code changes. In the context of graphics projects, CI plays a crucial role in ensuring code quality, stability, and compatibility across different platforms and configurations. This section explores the importance of CI in graphics development and provides insights into setting up CI pipelines for your projects.

1. Benefits of CI for Graphics Projects

CI offers several benefits for graphics development:

- **Early Issue Detection**: CI systems automatically build and test code changes, allowing you to detect issues early in the development cycle.

- **Cross-Platform Testing**: Graphics applications often target multiple platforms (Windows, macOS, Linux, consoles, etc.). CI pipelines enable you to test your code on various platforms and configurations.

- **Consistency**: CI ensures that every code change is built and tested in a consistent environment, reducing the "it works on my machine" problem.

- **Automated Testing**: You can set up automated tests, including rendering tests and performance benchmarks, as part of your CI pipeline.

2. Setting Up a CI Pipeline

To establish a CI pipeline for your graphics project, follow these steps:

2.1. Choose a CI Service

Select a CI service that suits your needs. Popular options include Travis CI, CircleCI, Jenkins, and GitLab CI/CD. These services provide infrastructure for building and testing your code automatically.

2.2. Repository Integration

Integrate your code repository (e.g., GitHub, GitLab, Bitbucket) with the chosen CI service. This integration allows the CI system to monitor your repository for changes.

2.3. Configuration File

Create a configuration file (e.g., .travis.yml for Travis CI) in your repository. This file specifies the build environment, dependencies, and testing instructions for your project.

2.4. Automated Builds

Set up automated builds that compile your graphics application. Ensure that your build scripts are platform-agnostic and can run on the CI service's infrastructure.

2.5. Automated Testing

Define automated tests that cover various aspects of your graphics application, such as rendering correctness, performance, and stability. These tests should run automatically on the CI service.

2.6. Cross-Platform Testing

If your project targets multiple platforms, configure the CI pipeline to build and test your code on each target platform. Use virtual machines or containers to replicate different environments.

2.7. Integration Tests

Include integration tests that validate interactions between different components of your graphics application, ensuring that they work together seamlessly.

3. Rendering Tests

For graphics projects, rendering tests are particularly important. These tests compare rendered frames against reference images to detect visual regressions. Consider the following when implementing rendering tests in your CI pipeline:

3.1. Reference Images

Store reference images in your repository or a dedicated storage location. These images represent the expected output of your graphics application.

3.2. Automated Comparison

Set up automated image comparison tools that compare rendered frames to reference images. Any differences should trigger a test failure.

3.3. Tolerance Thresholds

Define tolerance thresholds for image comparisons to account for minor rendering variations due to different hardware or drivers.

3.4. Continuous Monitoring

Regularly review rendering test results to identify and address visual regressions promptly.

4. Performance Benchmarks

In addition to correctness tests, consider incorporating performance benchmarks into your CI pipeline. These benchmarks help you monitor the performance impact of code changes over time.

5. Deployment

CI pipelines can also automate deployment processes. Depending on your project, you can configure your pipeline to deploy builds to various platforms or distribution channels automatically.

6. Conclusion

Continuous Integration is a powerful practice that enhances code quality, stability, and collaboration in graphics development. By setting up a CI pipeline tailored to your project's needs, you can ensure that your graphics application remains robust and performs optimally across diverse environments.

Section 16.3: Shader and Asset Pipelining

Shader and asset pipelining is a crucial aspect of graphics development, allowing you to efficiently manage and optimize the compilation and loading of shaders and assets in your project. In this section, we'll explore the importance of shader and asset pipelining, techniques for optimization, and best practices.

1. The Role of Pipelining

Pipelining refers to the process of organizing tasks in a way that allows for efficient execution and minimizes idle time. In graphics development, pipelining plays a significant role in optimizing shader compilation and asset loading, as both are performance-critical operations.

2. Shader Pipelining

2.1. Precompiled Shaders

Precompiled shaders can significantly reduce loading times and runtime compilation overhead. By precompiling shaders offline, you avoid the need for runtime compilation, which can be slow and introduce frame hitches.

2.2. Shader Caching

Implement a shader cache system that stores compiled shaders on disk. When your application starts, check the cache for precompiled shaders before compiling them again. This can greatly improve startup times.

2.3. Hot Reloading

For development purposes, consider implementing hot-reloading of shaders. This allows developers to edit and see changes to shaders in real-time without restarting the application. Be sure to handle shader recompilation gracefully to avoid crashes.

3. Asset Pipelining

3.1. Texture Compression

Use texture compression formats (e.g., BCn formats on DirectX, ETC formats on OpenGL) to reduce the size of textures without sacrificing quality. Compressed textures load faster and consume less memory.

3.2. Mipmapping

Generate mipmaps for textures. Mipmapping improves texture sampling performance and reduces aliasing artifacts. Many graphics APIs provide automatic mipmap generation.

3.3. Streaming

For large assets, like 3D models or terrain data, implement streaming techniques. Load only the portions of assets needed for the current view, and progressively load additional data as the camera moves.

3.4. Asset Bundling

Bundle related assets together to minimize the number of file I/O operations during loading. This can also help reduce load times.

3.5. Asynchronous Loading

Use asynchronous loading techniques to load assets in the background while your application continues running. This prevents frame hitches due to asset loading.

4. Build Pipelines

To streamline the process of shader and asset pipelining, consider implementing build pipelines:

4.1. Shader Build Pipeline

Create a build pipeline that automatically compiles shaders from source files. This pipeline can generate both precompiled shaders and shader reflection data for runtime use.

4.2. Asset Build Pipeline

Build pipelines can preprocess and optimize assets for runtime use. For example, they can compress textures, convert asset formats, or generate optimized meshes.

4.3. Version Control Integration

Integrate your build pipelines with version control systems to ensure consistency across development environments.

5. Cross-Platform Considerations

When implementing shader and asset pipelines, consider the platform-specific requirements of your target platforms. Some platforms may have unique shader formats or asset loading constraints.

6. Testing and Profiling

Thoroughly test and profile your shader and asset pipelines to identify bottlenecks and areas for optimization. Profiling tools can help pinpoint performance issues.

7. Conclusion

Efficient shader and asset pipelining are essential for optimizing the loading and compilation of graphics resources in your project. By adopting the practices and techniques mentioned in this section, you can significantly improve the performance and responsiveness of your graphics application while maintaining a smooth development workflow.

Section 16.4: Live Coding and Hot Reloading

Live coding and hot reloading are essential tools for graphics developers, enabling rapid iteration and testing of shaders and code during development without the need to restart the entire application. In this section, we'll explore the benefits, implementation strategies, and best practices of live coding and hot reloading in graphics programming.

1. The Benefits of Live Coding

Live coding provides several advantages during the development process:

- **Faster Iteration**: Developers can make changes to code or shaders and immediately see the results without waiting for compilation or application restarts.

- **Reduced Downtime**: Avoiding frequent restarts improves productivity by minimizing downtime caused by reloading assets or rebuilding shaders.

- **Real-time Debugging**: Debugging can be performed in real-time, making it easier to identify and fix issues as they arise.

2. Implementing Live Coding

2.1. Shader Hot Reloading

Shader hot reloading is a common use case for live coding. Here's how to implement it:

- **Monitor Shader Files**: Continuously monitor shader source files for changes.

- **Recompile Shaders**: When changes are detected, recompile the affected shaders.

- **Link Shaders**: Link the updated shaders into the rendering pipeline.

- **Replace Shaders**: Replace the old shaders with the newly compiled versions.

- **Graceful Handling**: Handle shader recompilation errors gracefully to avoid application crashes.

2.2. Code Hot Reloading

Hot reloading for code involves similar principles:

- **Monitor Source Files**: Continuously monitor code source files for changes.

- **Recompile Code**: Recompile the modified code.

- **Reload Modules**: Replace the old code modules with the newly compiled ones.

- **Maintain State**: Preserve application state as much as possible during code reloading to provide a seamless experience.

3. Best Practices

3.1. Granularity

Implement live coding for individual shaders or code modules rather than the entire application. This allows you to focus on specific parts of the project without affecting unrelated components.

3.2. Version Control

Use version control systems to track changes to shaders and code. This helps identify when and what changes were made and simplifies collaboration in team projects.

3.3. User Interface

Provide a user interface for enabling or disabling live coding features. This allows developers to control when and how live coding is applied.

3.4. Error Handling

Implement robust error handling for live coding scenarios. Inform developers of compilation errors and provide detailed error messages to expedite debugging.

3.5. Performance Profiling

Monitor the performance impact of live coding and hot reloading. While these features are invaluable during development, they can introduce performance overhead, so it's essential to profile and optimize when necessary.

4. Conclusion

Live coding and hot reloading are powerful tools that can significantly improve the efficiency and effectiveness of graphics development. By following best practices and implementing these features judiciously, developers can create more responsive and productive workflows, leading to better graphics applications.

Section 16.5: Collaborative Tools and Techniques

Collaboration is a fundamental aspect of graphics development, whether you're working on a small indie game or a large-scale AAA title. In this section, we'll explore collaborative tools and techniques that can streamline the development process and help teams work more efficiently together.

1. Version Control Systems

Version control systems (VCS) are essential for collaborative graphics projects. They allow multiple developers to work on the same codebase simultaneously while tracking changes and providing a history of revisions. Git, Mercurial, and Subversion are popular VCS choices in the graphics development community.

Best Practices for VCS:

- **Branching Strategy**: Establish a clear branching strategy to manage features, bug fixes, and experimental work.

- **Commit Frequently**: Encourage developers to commit code regularly to avoid conflicts and keep the codebase up-to-date.

- **Code Review**: Use pull requests or code review tools to ensure code quality and consistency.

2. Collaborative Coding Platforms

Collaborative coding platforms like GitHub, GitLab, and Bitbucket facilitate code sharing, collaboration, and issue tracking. These platforms provide a central repository for your graphics project, making it accessible to team members worldwide.

Key Features of Collaborative Coding Platforms:

- **Issue Tracking**: Create and manage issues, track feature requests, and prioritize tasks.

- **Pull Requests**: Review and approve changes made by team members before merging them into the main codebase.

- **Wikis and Documentation**: Maintain project documentation and wikis to ensure everyone has access to essential information.

3. Communication Tools

Effective communication is vital for distributed teams in graphics development. Use tools like Slack, Microsoft Teams, or Discord to facilitate real-time communication, share updates, and hold meetings. Video conferencing and screen sharing can be particularly valuable for discussing visual elements of the project.

Best Practices for Communication:

- **Regular Standup Meetings**: Conduct regular standup meetings to keep the team in sync and address any roadblocks.

- **Shared Channels**: Create dedicated channels or chat rooms for specific topics or teams within your project.

4. Asset Management

Graphics development often involves handling a vast number of assets, including textures, models, animations, and shaders. Effective asset management is crucial to ensure assets are organized, versioned, and accessible to team members.

Asset Management Tips:

- **Asset Naming Conventions**: Establish clear naming conventions for assets to prevent naming conflicts and ensure consistency.

- **Versioning**: Use version control for non-code assets, or consider specialized asset management tools.

- **Backup and Archiving**: Regularly back up assets, and consider archiving older versions to save storage space.

5. Remote Collaboration

Remote collaboration tools like Trello, Asana, or JIRA can help manage project tasks, timelines, and workflows. These tools allow teams to assign tasks, track progress, and set priorities, ensuring that development stays on schedule.

Remote Collaboration Best Practices:

- **Task Breakdown**: Divide complex tasks into smaller, manageable subtasks to facilitate collaboration and tracking.

- **Deadlines and Milestones**: Set clear deadlines and milestones to keep the project on track and monitor progress.

- **Regular Updates**: Provide regular updates on task status to keep team members informed.

6. Conclusion

Collaborative tools and techniques are essential for graphics development teams to work together efficiently and produce high-quality projects. By leveraging version control, collaborative coding platforms, communication tools, asset management, and remote collaboration solutions, developers and teams can streamline their workflows, enhance productivity, and deliver outstanding graphics experiences to users.

Chapter 17: Integrating Emerging Technologies

Section 17.1: Quantum Computing and Graphics

In recent years, quantum computing has emerged as a groundbreaking technology with the potential to revolutionize various fields, including graphics and simulation. While quantum computers are still in their infancy, it's essential to understand how they might impact graphics development and what opportunities they offer for improving rendering, simulation, and other graphics-related tasks.

Understanding Quantum Computing Basics

Before diving into quantum computing's implications for graphics, let's briefly explore some fundamental concepts:

Quantum Bits (Qubits):

Unlike classical bits that represent either 0 or 1, qubits can exist in a superposition of states, allowing for parallel processing and complex computations.

Quantum Entanglement:

Entangled qubits share a strong correlation, even when separated by large distances. Changes to one qubit instantaneously affect its entangled partner, enabling faster communication and synchronization.

Quantum Algorithms:

Quantum computers use quantum algorithms like Shor's algorithm and Grover's algorithm to solve specific problems exponentially faster than classical computers.

Quantum Computing in Graphics

While quantum computing is still in the experimental stage, its potential applications in graphics are promising:

1. Optimization:

Quantum computers excel at solving complex optimization problems. In graphics, this could translate to more efficient rendering, better pathfinding in games, and enhanced procedural content generation.

2. Quantum Simulations:

Quantum computers could simulate physical phenomena with unprecedented accuracy and speed. This might lead to more realistic simulations of fluid dynamics, particle systems, and materials in real-time graphics.

3. Quantum Machine Learning:

Quantum machine learning algorithms could improve AI-driven animations, enhance texture generation, and accelerate content creation in graphics.

4. Security:

Quantum computing also has implications for security. Graphics applications that rely on encryption and secure communication may need to adapt to quantum-safe encryption methods.

Challenges and Limitations

It's essential to recognize that quantum computing is still in its infancy, and several challenges need to be overcome:

Hardware Limitations:

Quantum computers are currently limited in terms of stability, error rates, and the number of qubits. Practical applications in graphics may require more powerful and stable quantum hardware.

Algorithm Development:

Developing quantum algorithms for specific graphics tasks will be a complex and evolving field, requiring collaboration between quantum scientists and graphics researchers.

Integration:

Integrating quantum computing into existing graphics pipelines and software frameworks will be a significant undertaking, requiring new software tools and development practices.

Conclusion

Quantum computing holds tremendous potential for graphics, offering the prospect of faster simulations, enhanced rendering, and improved AI-driven content creation. However, it's crucial to recognize that quantum computing is still in its early stages, and practical applications in graphics may take years to materialize. Graphics developers and researchers should stay informed about quantum computing advancements and be prepared to explore its potential as the technology matures.

Section 17.2: Integrating Biometrics in Games

As technology continues to advance, integrating biometrics into video games has become an intriguing area of exploration. Biometrics involves the measurement and analysis of a person's physical and behavioral characteristics. This section explores the potential applications, benefits, and challenges of integrating biometric data into gaming experiences.

Understanding Biometrics

Biometrics encompasses a wide range of data, including:

- **Facial Recognition:** Analyzing a player's facial features and expressions.

- **Heart Rate and Pulse:** Monitoring a player's heart rate during gameplay.

- **Eye Tracking:** Observing where a player looks on the screen.

- **Voice Analysis:** Analyzing a player's voice pitch, tone, and patterns.

- **Gaze Tracking:** Measuring the direction of a player's gaze.

- **Electrodermal Activity (EDA):** Monitoring changes in skin conductance due to emotional responses.

Potential Applications

1. Personalized Experiences:

By analyzing biometric data, games can adapt in real-time to a player's emotional state, providing challenges, rewards, or story elements tailored to their current mood.

2. Health and Well-being:

Biometric sensors can encourage physical activity in exergaming or alert players to take breaks when fatigue or stress levels rise.

3. Emotional Storytelling:

Games can adjust character interactions and narrative choices based on a player's emotional responses, creating more immersive and emotionally engaging stories.

4. Player Identification:

Biometrics can be used for player identification, enabling secure access to in-game accounts and personalized profiles.

Benefits

1. Enhanced Immersion:

Biometric data can help create more immersive and emotionally resonant gaming experiences by reacting to a player's emotional cues.

2. Health Benefits:

Games can promote physical and mental well-being by encouraging players to maintain healthy heart rates, reduce stress, or engage in relaxation exercises.

3. Personalization:

Games can tailor gameplay experiences, difficulty levels, and storylines to match a player's emotional state and preferences.

Challenges and Considerations

1. Privacy Concerns:

Collecting and using biometric data raises significant privacy concerns. Developers must establish robust data protection measures and obtain informed consent from players.

2. Hardware Requirements:

Biometric integration may require specialized hardware, such as cameras, sensors, or wearable devices, which can limit accessibility.

3. Ethical Considerations:

Developers should consider ethical issues related to biometric data, including consent, data ownership, and potential misuse.

4. Technical Challenges:

Analyzing biometric data in real-time and incorporating it into gameplay mechanics can be technically challenging, requiring expertise in data analysis and game design.

Conclusion

Integrating biometrics into games has the potential to revolutionize player experiences by creating more immersive and personalized gameplay. However, developers must navigate complex ethical, privacy, and technical challenges while ensuring that the integration of biometric data enhances, rather than compromises, the gaming experience. As technology continues to evolve, the role of biometrics in gaming is likely to expand, providing new opportunities for innovation and player engagement.

Section 17.3: Brain-computer Interfaces

Brain-computer interfaces (BCIs) represent a fascinating and evolving field of technology that holds immense promise for the future of gaming. These interfaces establish direct communication between the human brain and external devices or systems, offering unique opportunities for more immersive and interactive gaming experiences. In this section, we explore the principles, potential applications, and challenges associated with integrating brain-computer interfaces into gaming.

How Brain-Computer Interfaces Work

BCIs function by detecting and interpreting electrical signals generated by the brain. These signals are typically measured through electroencephalography (EEG), functional magnetic resonance imaging (fMRI), or other neuroimaging techniques. The data collected is then processed by specialized software to translate brain activity into meaningful commands or actions that can be used in gaming.

Potential Applications in Gaming

1. Mind-Controlled Gameplay:

One of the most exciting prospects of BCIs in gaming is the ability to control in-game actions using thoughts alone. Players can move characters, trigger abilities, or make decisions simply by thinking about them.

2. Enhanced Immersion:

BCIs can be used to monitor a player's emotional state or engagement level, allowing the game to dynamically adjust difficulty, pacing, or story elements for a more immersive experience.

3. Accessibility:

BCIs have the potential to make gaming more accessible to individuals with physical disabilities, allowing them to enjoy games and interact with virtual worlds using their thoughts.

4. Neurofeedback:

Games can provide real-time feedback on a player's brain activity, encouraging relaxation or focus, and training cognitive skills.

Benefits of Brain-Computer Interfaces in Gaming

1. Accessibility and Inclusion:

BCIs can break down barriers for players with disabilities, enabling them to engage with games in ways that were previously impossible.

2. Immersive Experiences:

By directly tapping into a player's thoughts and emotions, BCIs can create incredibly immersive and emotionally resonant gaming experiences.

3. Personalization:

Games can adapt to a player's cognitive state and preferences, tailoring challenges, rewards, and storylines accordingly.

Challenges and Considerations

1. Technical Complexity:

Developing BCIs for gaming requires expertise in neurology, signal processing, and software development, making it a technically challenging endeavor.

2. Privacy and Ethical Concerns:

Collecting and interpreting brain data raises significant privacy and ethical questions, necessitating stringent data protection measures and informed consent.

3. Adoption and Cost:

The widespread adoption of BCIs in gaming may be limited by factors such as cost, availability, and the need for specialized hardware.

4. Learning Curve:

Players may need time to adapt to controlling games with their thoughts, and not everyone may find this mode of interaction intuitive or enjoyable.

Future Possibilities

As BCIs continue to advance, the possibilities for their integration into gaming are bound to expand. Developers and researchers are exploring innovative ways to harness this technology, opening doors to new forms of gameplay, enhanced storytelling, and greater accessibility. While challenges remain, the potential benefits of BCIs in gaming are too significant to ignore, promising a future where players can immerse themselves in virtual worlds like never before.

Section 17.4: Graphics for Advanced Robotics

The intersection of graphics technology and robotics has opened up exciting possibilities in various fields, from manufacturing and healthcare to entertainment and research. In this section, we explore the role of advanced graphics techniques in robotics and how they contribute to the development and operation of sophisticated robotic systems.

Simulation and Training

Graphics play a pivotal role in simulating real-world environments for robotic training and testing. Advanced physics engines and rendering technologies allow researchers and engineers to create highly realistic virtual environments where robots can be trained to perform tasks, refine their algorithms, and adapt to various scenarios. These simulations are crucial for both industrial and research robots, helping reduce the risk of accidents during development and enabling robots to be better prepared for real-world challenges.

Visual SLAM (Simultaneous Localization and Mapping)

Visual Simultaneous Localization and Mapping (SLAM) is a vital component of robotics, enabling robots to understand and navigate their surroundings. Advanced graphics techniques, including computer vision, depth sensing, and 3D mapping, are used to create detailed and accurate representations of the environment. This information is essential for a robot's ability to navigate autonomously, avoid obstacles, and perform tasks effectively. Graphics technology ensures that robots can perceive and interpret their surroundings with precision.

Human-Robot Interaction

In applications where robots interact with humans, such as service robots or collaborative robots (cobots), realistic and intuitive interfaces are crucial. Graphics technology helps create lifelike avatars, graphical user interfaces, and augmented reality (AR) overlays that facilitate natural and effective communication between humans and robots. These interfaces enhance the user experience and make human-robot collaboration more seamless and efficient.

Data Visualization and Analysis

Robotic systems generate vast amounts of data during their operation. Graphics techniques are employed to visualize and analyze this data, making it comprehensible and actionable for researchers, engineers, and operators. Whether it's tracking the movement of autonomous vehicles, monitoring sensor data in real time, or visualizing the results of experiments, advanced graphics capabilities enable efficient data processing and decision-making.

Advanced Control Interfaces

Graphics technology is leveraged to create advanced control interfaces for robots, especially in fields like teleoperation and telepresence. These interfaces provide operators with immersive views of a robot's surroundings, often in 3D or VR environments, allowing for precise control and a sense of presence. This is particularly valuable in situations where human dexterity and judgment are required, such as remote surgery or hazardous environment exploration.

Challenges and Considerations

While the integration of graphics technology and robotics offers many advantages, there are challenges to overcome:

1. **Real-Time Processing:** Robotics demands real-time processing, which can be computationally intensive. Ensuring low latency and high performance in graphics

processing is crucial for robotic applications.

2. **Data Integration:** Combining data from various sensors and sources, including cameras, lidar, and other sensors, can be complex. Effective integration and synchronization of data are essential for accurate robot perception.

3. **Safety:** In scenarios where robots operate alongside humans, safety is paramount. Graphics technology must be designed with safety considerations in mind to prevent accidents and ensure human-robot interaction is secure.

4. **Scalability:** Graphics systems must be scalable to accommodate the increasing complexity of robotic tasks and environments, which may involve more sensors, robots, and data sources.

Future Outlook

The synergy between graphics technology and robotics continues to drive innovation in both fields. As graphics hardware and software capabilities advance, robots will become more sophisticated, capable of performing complex tasks in diverse environments. The fusion of graphics and robotics holds immense potential for revolutionizing industries, improving healthcare, and enabling new forms of entertainment and exploration. It's an exciting frontier where creative applications of graphics technology are shaping the future of robotics.

Section 17.5: Evolution of Wearable Tech

Wearable technology, often referred to as wearables, has been a rapidly evolving field that has implications for both personal and professional use cases. In this section, we will delve into the evolution of wearable tech, exploring its origins, current state, and potential future directions.

The Birth of Wearable Tech

Wearable technology is not a new concept. In fact, it can be traced back to the earliest inventions like the pocket watch and eyeglasses. However, the modern era of wearables began in the late 20th century when electronic devices started to be integrated into clothing and accessories. For example, early iterations included calculator watches and simple fitness trackers.

Fitness and Health Tracking

One of the primary drivers of wearable technology adoption has been fitness and health tracking. Wearable fitness trackers and smartwatches have gained immense popularity due to their ability to monitor physical activity, heart rate, sleep patterns, and more. They have evolved to become comprehensive health and wellness companions, providing insights and actionable data to users.

Smartwatches and Beyond

Smartwatches represent a significant milestone in wearable tech evolution. They are no longer just timekeeping devices but serve as extensions of smartphones. Smartwatches enable users to receive notifications, make calls, send messages, and even run apps directly from their wrists. Their functionality continues to expand with each new generation.

Augmented Reality (AR) Glasses

Augmented reality glasses like Google Glass and Microsoft HoloLens have introduced a new dimension to wearable technology. They overlay digital information onto the real world, making them valuable tools for industries like manufacturing, healthcare, and education. The potential for AR glasses in gaming and entertainment is also being explored.

Virtual Reality (VR) Headsets

While not as commonly worn throughout the day, VR headsets are a significant category within wearable tech. They offer immersive experiences for gaming, training, simulations, and virtual travel. The VR industry continues to advance, with high-quality headsets becoming more accessible to consumers.

Future Directions

The future of wearable tech holds exciting possibilities:

1. **Healthcare Revolution:** Wearables will continue to play a pivotal role in healthcare, with advancements in remote patient monitoring, early disease detection, and personalized treatment recommendations.
2. **Extended Reality (XR):** The convergence of AR and VR, known as Extended Reality (XR), will lead to more versatile devices that can seamlessly switch between augmented and virtual environments.
3. **Fashion and Style:** Wearable technology will become more integrated with fashion, blurring the lines between tech gadgets and clothing/accessories. Aesthetics and wearability will be key considerations.
4. **Brain-Computer Interfaces (BCI):** The development of BCIs will enable direct communication between the human brain and wearable devices, opening up new possibilities for controlling tech with our thoughts.
5. **Eco-Friendly Wearables:** As sustainability becomes a priority, eco-friendly materials and energy-efficient designs

will shape the next generation of wearables.

Ethical and Privacy Considerations

The widespread adoption of wearables also raises important ethical and privacy concerns. Data security, consent, and the responsible use of personal information are topics that need careful attention as wearables become more ingrained in our daily lives.

In conclusion, wearable technology has come a long way from its humble beginnings, and its journey is far from over. As technology continues to advance, wearables will continue to evolve, becoming more integrated into our lives and potentially revolutionizing industries and the way we interact with the digital world.

Chapter 18: Open Standards and Future Graphics APIs

Section 18.1: Beyond OpenGL: Vulkan and DirectX

In the world of graphics programming, APIs (Application Programming Interfaces) play a crucial role in bridging the gap between software and hardware, allowing developers to harness the power of modern GPUs. In this section, we will explore the evolution of graphics APIs, focusing on two significant players: Vulkan and DirectX.

The Legacy of OpenGL

For many years, OpenGL was the dominant graphics API, offering a cross-platform solution for rendering 2D and 3D graphics. It provided a standard way for developers to interact with GPUs, making it possible to create visually stunning applications and games on a wide range of devices and operating systems.

However, as hardware and software evolved, OpenGL began to show its age. Its design, which originated in the early days of fixed-function graphics pipelines, was not well-suited to the demands of modern real-time graphics. Developers often had to write complex and verbose code to achieve the desired visual effects, and performance optimization was a constant challenge.

Enter Vulkan

Vulkan emerged as the next-generation graphics API to address the limitations of OpenGL. It was developed by the Khronos Group, the same consortium behind OpenGL, but with a fresh perspective and a focus on modern GPU architectures.

Vulkan provides low-level, explicit control over GPU resources and parallelism, allowing developers to squeeze every ounce of performance from their hardware. It offers a more efficient and scalable approach to graphics rendering, making it suitable for a wide range of applications, from games to professional graphics software.

One of Vulkan's key features is its multi-threading support, which enables developers to leverage the full power of multi-core CPUs. This is crucial for achieving high frame rates and smooth gameplay experiences in modern games.

DirectX: Microsoft's Offering

On the Windows platform, Microsoft's DirectX has long been a popular choice for game developers. Like Vulkan, DirectX has evolved over the years to keep pace with advancements in GPU technology.

DirectX 12, in particular, introduced several features that align with Vulkan's design principles, such as low-level access to GPU resources and improved multi-threading support. This made it more competitive in the realm of high-performance graphics.

Choosing the Right API

The choice between Vulkan and DirectX often depends on the target platform and development preferences. Vulkan's cross-platform nature makes it an attractive option for developers who want to reach a wide audience, including Windows, Linux, Android, and more.

DirectX, on the other hand, remains the primary choice for Windows game development, especially for titles targeting the Xbox platform. Additionally, DirectX's integration with other Microsoft technologies can be advantageous for Windows-centric development.

Ultimately, the decision should align with your project's goals and requirements. Both Vulkan and DirectX offer powerful tools for graphics programming, and mastering either API can open doors to exciting opportunities in the world of real-time rendering.

In the next sections of this chapter, we will delve deeper into the specifics of Vulkan, DirectX, and the broader landscape of graphics APIs, exploring how they work and how to leverage their features to create stunning visual experiences. Whether you're a seasoned graphics programmer or just starting your journey, this chapter will provide valuable insights into the future of graphics programming.

Section 18.2: Open Standards in the Graphics World

In the world of computer graphics, open standards play a crucial role in ensuring interoperability, innovation, and accessibility across a wide range of applications and platforms. These standards define common protocols and formats, allowing developers to create software and content that can run on diverse hardware and operating systems. In this section, we will explore the importance of open standards in the graphics industry and their impact on the development of graphics applications and APIs.

The Role of Open Standards

Open standards are specifications or protocols that are publicly available and not controlled by any single entity. They are designed to promote transparency, collaboration, and fair competition in the technology industry. In the context of graphics, open standards help ensure that graphics content and applications can be created, shared, and experienced seamlessly across different devices and software platforms.

OpenGL and Its Impact

OpenGL, one of the most well-known open graphics standards, has had a profound influence on the graphics industry. Initially released in the early 1990s, OpenGL provided a consistent and cross-platform way to interact with GPUs, making it possible to create graphics applications that could run on various operating systems.

Over the years, OpenGL's open nature has encouraged collaboration and innovation. It has been adapted and extended by many hardware and software vendors to support advanced graphics features, making it a versatile choice for game developers, 3D artists, and scientific visualization applications.

Vulkan: A Modern Open Standard

Vulkan, developed by the Khronos Group, is another example of an open graphics standard that has gained traction in recent years. Vulkan's design principles focus on providing low-level, explicit control over GPU resources and parallelism, allowing developers to achieve high performance and efficiency.

Vulkan's open standard status means that it can be implemented on various platforms, including Windows, Linux, and Android. This versatility has made Vulkan an attractive choice for developers looking to target a wide range of devices and operating systems while maintaining a consistent graphics codebase.

Web Graphics and Open Standards

The web is a critical platform for graphics content delivery, and open standards are instrumental in ensuring that graphics are accessible and interactive across web browsers. Technologies like HTML5, WebGL, and WebGPU rely on open standards to define how graphics and multimedia content are presented and manipulated within web pages.

HTML5 introduced the <canvas> element, which allows developers to draw graphics and animations directly on web pages using JavaScript. WebGL, based on the OpenGL ES standard, provides a low-level API for 3D graphics rendering within web browsers. WebGPU is an emerging standard designed to provide even lower-level access to GPU capabilities, enabling high-performance web graphics and compute tasks.

Interoperability and Cross-Platform Development

Open standards enable interoperability, allowing content and applications to work seamlessly across different platforms and devices. This is particularly important in today's diverse computing landscape, where users may access graphics content on PCs, mobile devices, game consoles, and more.

Developers can leverage open standards to create cross-platform graphics applications, reducing the effort required to adapt their software to various environments. This approach not only saves time and resources but also broadens the reach of their applications to a wider audience.

Conclusion

Open standards have played a pivotal role in the evolution of computer graphics, fostering innovation, collaboration, and accessibility. They have enabled developers to create graphics applications and content that can run on a diverse range of hardware and software platforms. Whether you are developing games, simulations, or visualization tools, understanding and embracing open standards can be a key factor in the success of your graphics projects. In the next sections of this chapter, we will continue to explore the landscape of open standards in graphics, including the evolving world of web graphics and the potential of cross-API techniques and tools.

Section 18.3: The Evolution of Web Graphics

The web has become an integral part of our daily lives, and as a result, the demand for rich and interactive web graphics has grown significantly. In this section, we will explore the evolution of web graphics and the technologies that have played a crucial role in delivering visually engaging content on the web.

Early Web Graphics

In the early days of the World Wide Web, web graphics were primarily limited to simple images and text. Web pages were static, and animations or interactive graphics were rare. These graphics were typically in formats like GIF and JPEG, which were well-suited for photographs and basic illustrations.

Flash and Interactive Multimedia

Macromedia Flash, later acquired by Adobe, was a revolutionary technology that brought interactive multimedia to the web. Flash allowed developers to create animations, games, and interactive applications that ran directly in web browsers. It introduced vector graphics, which could scale without loss of quality, and a scripting language (ActionScript) for interactivity.

Flash content was widely used for web-based games, multimedia presentations, and even entire websites. However, it had drawbacks, including performance issues, security vulnerabilities, and limited support on mobile devices. Over time, these limitations led to a decline in Flash usage.

HTML5 and Canvas

HTML5, along with the <canvas> element and JavaScript, marked a significant shift in web graphics development. The <canvas> element allowed developers to draw 2D graphics directly on web pages using JavaScript. This opened the door to creating interactive graphics, animations, and even games without the need for plugins like Flash.

Canvas-based web graphics became a popular choice for game development, data visualization, and interactive infographics. JavaScript libraries and frameworks like Three.js and PixiJS made it easier for developers to work with <canvas> and create sophisticated web graphics applications.

WebGL for 3D Graphics

WebGL, based on the OpenGL ES standard, brought 3D graphics capabilities to web browsers. It allowed developers to create 3D scenes, render models, and apply shaders directly within web pages. WebGL leveraged the GPU for hardware-accelerated rendering, enabling impressive 3D graphics on the web.

With the advent of WebGL, web-based 3D games, simulations, and visualizations became feasible. Frameworks like Babylon.js and A-Frame made it easier to work with WebGL, making 3D web graphics accessible to a broader audience.

WebGPU and Future Prospects

WebGPU is an emerging web graphics standard designed to provide even lower-level access to GPU capabilities within web browsers. It aims to unlock even greater performance and efficiency for web graphics and compute tasks.

WebGPU is still in development, but it holds promise for the future of web graphics. It will enable developers to harness the full power of modern GPUs directly in web applications, potentially opening up new possibilities for immersive web experiences and complex simulations.

Conclusion

The evolution of web graphics has been marked by a transition from static images to interactive and 3D experiences. HTML5, Canvas, WebGL, and the upcoming WebGPU standard have all contributed to making web graphics more powerful and accessible. As web technologies continue to advance, we can expect web graphics to play an increasingly significant role in delivering engaging content and applications on the web. This evolution underscores the importance of staying up-to-date with web graphics technologies for developers and content creators alike.

Section 18.4: Cross-API Techniques and Tools

In the world of graphics programming, different graphics APIs (Application Programming Interfaces) have been developed over the years to interact with GPUs. These APIs serve as a bridge between software and hardware, enabling developers to create stunning visuals and real-time simulations. In this section, we'll explore cross-API techniques and tools that allow graphics developers to work efficiently across multiple graphics APIs.

The Challenge of Multiple Graphics APIs

Graphics developers often face the challenge of dealing with various graphics APIs, each with its own syntax, capabilities, and quirks. For example, DirectX is commonly used on Windows, while Vulkan and OpenGL are cross-platform APIs. Game engines and applications may need to support multiple APIs to reach a broader audience.

Abstraction Layers

One approach to dealing with multiple APIs is to use abstraction layers or libraries that provide a unified interface. These layers hide the API-specific details, allowing developers to write code that works across different platforms and APIs. Popular libraries like GLFW, SDL, and Qt help in managing windows, input, and other aspects of graphics development.

Graphics Middleware

Graphics middleware solutions like NVIDIA's NVAPI and AMD's AGS provide tools and libraries for developers to optimize their graphics applications for specific hardware and APIs. These middleware solutions offer performance enhancements, debugging tools, and hardware-specific features to fine-tune graphics applications.

High-Level Graphics APIs

High-level graphics APIs, such as Apple's Metal and Microsoft's DirectML, abstract the complexities of lower-level APIs like Vulkan and DirectX. They provide a more streamlined and user-friendly interface for developers, making it easier to create graphics-intensive applications while retaining some level of performance control.

Cross-API Compatibility Tools

Several tools and frameworks are designed explicitly to help developers work across multiple graphics APIs:

1. **MoltenVK**: This tool allows developers to run Vulkan applications on macOS and iOS, bridging the gap between Vulkan and Apple's Metal API.
2. **ANGLE (Almost Native Graphics Layer Engine)**: ANGLE is an open-source project that translates OpenGL ES calls into DirectX, Vulkan, or Metal, depending on the platform. This enables developers to write cross-platform applications using WebGL and other OpenGL ES-based technologies.
3. **gfx-rs**: A Rust project that aims to provide a unified graphics API for Rust applications while targeting various backends, including Vulkan, DirectX 12, and Metal.

Graphics API Translation Layers

Some projects aim to create translation layers that allow running applications designed for one API on another. For example, the Zink project translates OpenGL applications to Vulkan, providing an alternative route for OpenGL applications to run on platforms with limited or no native OpenGL support.

Conclusion

Cross-API techniques and tools are essential in the world of graphics programming, where compatibility and performance optimization can be complex challenges. Graphics developers must choose the right tools and strategies to ensure their applications run efficiently across a wide range of platforms and devices. As graphics APIs continue to evolve, these techniques and tools will play a crucial role in simplifying the development and deployment of graphics-intensive applications.

Section 18.5: The Future Landscape of Graphics Programming

The field of graphics programming has witnessed remarkable advancements over the years, driven by the continuous evolution of hardware, software, and the increasing demands of applications and industries that rely on cutting-edge graphics. In this final section, we will explore the future landscape of graphics programming, including emerging trends, challenges, and opportunities.

Real-time Ray Tracing

Real-time ray tracing is a game-changer in computer graphics, enabling incredibly realistic lighting, reflections, and shadows in real-time applications. As hardware support for ray tracing becomes more widespread and efficient, we can expect to see more applications and games leveraging this technology for immersive visual experiences.

Advanced AI Integration

Artificial intelligence and machine learning are becoming integral to graphics programming. AI-driven algorithms can enhance various aspects of graphics, including content generation, animation, optimization, and even real-time decision-making in games. We can anticipate further integration of AI into the graphics pipeline, leading to smarter and more dynamic graphics applications.

Real-time Volumetrics and Simulation

Volumetric rendering techniques, which model the behavior of light within a 3D space, are gaining prominence. These techniques are crucial for creating realistic atmospheric effects, smoke, fire, and other complex visual phenomena. As hardware capabilities improve, real-time volumetric rendering and simulation will become more accessible, revolutionizing the realism of graphics.

Cross-Platform and Cross-Reality Development

Developers are increasingly challenged to create applications that work seamlessly across diverse platforms, including traditional PCs, mobile devices, virtual reality (VR), augmented reality (AR), and mixed reality (MR) systems. The future of graphics programming involves more emphasis on cross-platform and cross-reality development to cater to a wider audience.

Quantum Computing in Graphics

Quantum computing is still in its infancy, but it holds immense potential for graphics programming. Quantum algorithms can potentially solve complex graphics problems, such as global illumination, optimization, and material simulation, much faster than classical computers. As quantum hardware matures, we may see quantum-accelerated graphics techniques emerging.

Ethical and Inclusive Design

With the growing awareness of ethical considerations and the importance of inclusivity, graphics programmers will need to prioritize responsible design. This includes addressing issues related to accessibility, diversity, privacy, and environmental impact in the development of graphics applications.

Web-Based Graphics

Web-based graphics are becoming increasingly sophisticated, with technologies like WebGPU and WebAssembly pushing the boundaries of what can be achieved in a browser. This trend is likely to continue, enabling high-performance graphics applications directly within web browsers.

Collaborative and Open-Source Development

Collaboration and open-source initiatives will remain vital in the world of graphics programming. Developers from diverse backgrounds and industries will continue to share knowledge, tools, and resources to advance the field collectively.

In conclusion, the future of graphics programming is promising, with exciting opportunities to explore. As technology evolves and new challenges arise, graphics developers will need to adapt, innovate, and embrace emerging trends to create the next generation of visually stunning and immersive experiences. The landscape of graphics programming will continue to evolve, making it an exciting and dynamic field for those passionate about pushing the boundaries of what's possible in computer graphics.

Chapter 19: Ethics, Accessibility, and Inclusion

Section 19.1: Designing for All Users

In the world of graphics programming, it's crucial to prioritize designing applications and experiences that are accessible and inclusive to all users. Accessibility in this context refers to making sure that individuals with disabilities can perceive, understand, navigate, and interact with graphics-based content effectively. Inclusion extends this concept by ensuring that graphics experiences are welcoming to diverse audiences, regardless of their background or characteristics.

The Importance of Accessibility

1. **Legal and Ethical Obligations:** Many countries have laws that mandate accessibility standards for digital content. Failing to comply with these laws can result in legal consequences. Beyond legal obligations, there is an ethical responsibility to ensure that everyone, regardless of their abilities, can access and enjoy digital content.

2. **Expanding the User Base:** Prioritizing accessibility broadens your potential user base. By making your graphics applications usable by individuals with disabilities, you open your product to a larger audience. This not only enhances inclusivity but can also have economic benefits.

3. **Innovation and Problem Solving:** Designing for accessibility often requires creative problem-solving. This innovation can lead to improvements in user experience for all users, not just those with disabilities. Constraints can drive creativity and result in more intuitive interfaces.

4. **Positive Brand Image:** Demonstrating a commitment to accessibility and inclusion can enhance your brand's image. Users are increasingly conscious of a company's values and practices, and being known as an inclusive and ethical developer can be a competitive advantage.

Key Considerations in Designing Accessible Graphics

1. **User-Centered Design:** Start by understanding your users. Consider various user personas, including those with disabilities. Involve individuals with disabilities in user testing and feedback to ensure that your graphics meet their needs.
2. **Accessible Content:** Ensure that all content, including images, videos, and interactive elements, is accessible to screen readers and assistive technologies. Use descriptive alt text for images, provide transcripts for videos, and ensure that interactive elements are keyboard-navigable.
3. **Color and Contrast:** Pay attention to color choices and contrast. Ensure that text is readable against background colors and that color is not the sole means of conveying information. Use patterns and other visual cues in addition to color.
4. **Font and Typography:** Choose fonts and typography that are legible and easy to read. Avoid decorative fonts for body text and consider the spacing between letters and lines to improve readability.
5. **Navigation and Interface:** Design a clear and logical navigation structure. Use headings, labels, and landmarks to help users understand the layout and flow of your graphics application.
6. **User Feedback and Error Handling:** Provide clear and

meaningful feedback to users, especially when errors occur. Ensure that error messages are understandable and offer guidance on how to correct issues.

7. **Testing and Validation:** Regularly test your graphics applications with accessibility tools and screen readers. Conduct usability testing with individuals who have disabilities to identify and address any usability issues.

8. **Continuous Improvement:** Accessibility is an ongoing process. As technologies evolve, continue to update and improve your graphics applications to ensure they remain accessible to all users.

Incorporating accessibility and inclusion into your graphics programming practices is not only a legal and ethical requirement but also a way to create more innovative and user-friendly experiences. By designing for all users, you can make a positive impact and contribute to a more inclusive digital landscape.

Section 19.2: Addressing Photosensitive Epilepsy Concerns

Photosensitive epilepsy is a condition in which exposure to certain visual stimuli, such as flashing lights or rapidly changing patterns, can trigger seizures in susceptible individuals. While this condition is relatively rare, it's essential for graphics programmers to be aware of it and take measures to minimize the risk of inducing seizures through their work.

Understanding the Risk

1. **Epilepsy Triggers:** Photosensitive epilepsy can be triggered by specific visual patterns or stimuli, including rapidly flashing lights, high-contrast patterns, and certain

color combinations. Seizures induced by these triggers are known as photosensitive seizures.

2. **Individual Variability:** Not all individuals with epilepsy are photosensitive, and the degree of sensitivity varies among those who are. It's challenging to predict who may be susceptible, so it's crucial to adopt preventive measures.

Mitigating Photosensitive Epilepsy Risks

As a graphics programmer, there are several steps you can take to reduce the risk of triggering photosensitive seizures in your applications and content:

1. **Avoid Rapid Flashes:** One of the most critical precautions is to avoid rapid, high-frequency flashing in your graphics. If your application includes animated sequences or transitions, ensure that they do not contain abrupt, high-contrast flashes.

2. **Limit Flashing Patterns:** Be cautious with repetitive patterns or sequences of lights. These can be problematic for photosensitive individuals. If such patterns are necessary for your graphics, consider reducing their frequency and intensity.

3. **Provide User Controls:** Whenever possible, give users control over visual effects in your applications. Allow them to adjust settings related to motion, flashes, and other potentially triggering elements. This empowers users to customize their experience to reduce risks.

4. **Implement Warnings:** Consider adding warnings or disclaimers to your graphics applications or content if they contain elements that may pose a photosensitive epilepsy risk. Inform users about potential triggers and advise them to proceed with caution.

5. **User Testing:** Conduct user testing, including individuals with epilepsy, to identify and address potential issues. Gather feedback and make necessary adjustments to minimize risks.

6. **Compliance with Standards:** Familiarize yourself with guidelines and standards related to photosensitive epilepsy prevention. For example, the Web Content Accessibility Guidelines (WCAG) provide recommendations for designing content that is less likely to induce seizures.

Testing for Photosensitive Epilepsy Risks

Testing for photosensitive epilepsy risks can be challenging, as the susceptibility varies among individuals. However, there are tools and guidelines available to help you assess your graphics for potential risks:

1. **Seizure Risk Assessment Tools:** Some software tools and online services can analyze your graphics or animations for photosensitive epilepsy risks. These tools can identify potentially problematic sequences.

2. **WCAG Guidelines:** The WCAG provides specific recommendations for preventing photosensitive seizures in web content. Adhering to these guidelines can help ensure your web-based graphics are safer for all users.

3. **User Feedback:** Encourage users to report any concerns related to photosensitive epilepsy risks. If users experience discomfort or adverse effects, take their feedback seriously and make necessary adjustments.

In conclusion, addressing photosensitive epilepsy concerns in graphics programming is essential to create a safe and inclusive user experience. By following guidelines, conducting testing, and being mindful of potential triggers, you can help ensure that your graphics applications and content are less likely to induce seizures in susceptible individuals.

Section 19.3: Ethical Considerations in Graphics Technology

The field of graphics technology has evolved rapidly, enabling stunning visual experiences and pushing the boundaries of what's possible in digital content creation. However, this progress also brings forth various ethical considerations that must be addressed by developers, designers, and policymakers. In this section, we will explore some of these ethical considerations and discuss strategies for responsible graphics technology development.

1. Representation and Diversity

When creating graphics content, it's essential to consider issues related to representation and diversity. Graphics, including characters, environments, and assets, should strive to represent a broad range of identities, cultures, and backgrounds. Failing to do so can perpetuate stereotypes and underrepresentation. Developers should actively seek to include diverse perspectives in their teams and engage with communities to ensure inclusive content creation.

2. Accessibility

Graphics technology can inadvertently exclude individuals with disabilities if not designed with accessibility in mind. Accessibility features, such as alternative text for images, keyboard navigation, and color contrast, should be integrated into graphics applications and content. Following accessibility standards, such as WCAG, helps ensure that graphics are usable by a more extensive range of users.

3. Privacy and Data Collection

Graphics applications often collect data from users, such as user behavior analytics and personal information. Ethical concerns arise when data collection is not transparent or when users' privacy rights are violated. Developers should be transparent about data collection practices, obtain user consent, and implement robust security measures to protect user data.

4. Algorithmic Bias

Algorithms used in graphics technology, such as those for image recognition or content recommendation, can exhibit bias, leading to unfair or discriminatory outcomes. Developers should continually audit and refine algorithms to minimize bias and ensure equitable results. Diverse training data and rigorous testing can help address this issue.

5. Environmental Impact

Graphics technology, particularly in the gaming industry, can have a significant environmental impact due to energy consumption from high-performance hardware. Ethical considerations include optimizing software for energy efficiency and promoting responsible consumption practices among users.

6. Copyright and Intellectual Property

Graphics technology often involves the use of copyrighted materials and intellectual property. Developers must respect copyright laws and obtain the necessary permissions for using third-party assets. Promoting respect for intellectual property rights is crucial in graphics technology.

7. Fake and Misleading Content

The rise of deepfake technology and advanced image manipulation tools poses ethical challenges. Developers and content creators should be mindful of the potential for misinformation and ensure that their work does not deceive or manipulate users in harmful ways.

8. Transparency and Accountability

Transparency is vital in graphics technology development. Developers should communicate openly about their intentions, practices, and ethical guidelines. Establishing mechanisms for accountability and user feedback can help address ethical concerns as they arise.

9. Social Responsibility

Graphics technology has a substantial impact on society and culture. Developers and creators should consider the potential consequences of their work on broader social issues. Engaging in discussions about the responsible use of graphics technology and its impact on society is essential.

In conclusion, ethical considerations are integral to the development and application of graphics technology. Developers and creators have a responsibility to prioritize diversity, accessibility, privacy, fairness, and transparency in their work. By addressing these ethical concerns, the graphics technology industry can contribute to a more inclusive, responsible, and socially aware digital landscape.

Section 19.4: Open Source and Community Contributions

Open source development and community contributions play a significant role in the field of graphics technology. In this section, we will explore the importance of open source projects, the benefits they offer, and how community contributions contribute to the advancement of graphics technology.

1. Collaborative Development

Open source graphics projects allow developers from around the world to collaborate on software and tools. This collaborative approach fosters innovation and accelerates development. Graphics technology projects often involve complex algorithms and optimizations, and the collective effort of a community can lead to more robust and efficient solutions.

2. Accessibility

Open source projects make graphics technology more accessible to a broader audience. They are often freely available and can be customized to suit specific needs. This accessibility lowers barriers to entry for developers and researchers interested in working with graphics technology, ultimately driving innovation.

3. Transparency and Trust

Open source projects are transparent, with their source code available for inspection. This transparency builds trust among users and contributors, as they can review the code to ensure it aligns with their needs and values. It also enables security audits to identify and address vulnerabilities.

4. Community Support

Open source communities provide valuable support to users and developers. Forums, mailing lists, and chat platforms allow individuals to seek help, share knowledge, and collaborate on problem-solving. This support network is especially beneficial for those new to graphics technology.

5. Learning Opportunities

Contributing to open source graphics projects offers valuable learning opportunities. Developers can gain hands-on experience, learn from experts, and improve their skills. This learning experience is not limited to coding but extends to project management, documentation, and communication.

6. Customization and Extensibility

Open source graphics projects are often designed with customization and extensibility in mind. Users can modify the software to suit their specific requirements or build extensions and plugins to enhance functionality. This flexibility is particularly valuable in graphics technology, where diverse needs exist.

7. Community Diversity

Open source communities are typically diverse, comprising individuals from various backgrounds, cultures, and skill levels. This diversity brings different perspectives and ideas to the table, leading to more creative and inclusive solutions in graphics technology.

8. Leveraging Existing Work

Open source projects build upon the work of others. Developers can leverage existing libraries, frameworks, and tools, saving time and effort. This collaborative approach reduces duplication of work and encourages the reuse of well-established components.

9. Contributing Back

When developers and organizations benefit from open source graphics technology, there is an expectation that they will contribute back to the community. This can take the form of code contributions, bug reports, documentation updates, or financial support for project maintainers.

10. Ethical Considerations

Open source development aligns with ethical principles of transparency and inclusivity. It promotes a culture of sharing and cooperation, fostering responsible and community-driven graphics technology.

In summary, open source and community contributions are essential drivers of innovation and progress in the field of graphics technology. They offer accessibility, transparency, and a supportive environment for developers and users alike. By actively participating in open source projects and contributing to the community, individuals and organizations can help shape the future of graphics technology in a positive and collaborative way.

Section 19.5: Ensuring Future Tech is Inclusive

As the field of graphics technology continues to advance, it's crucial to prioritize inclusivity to ensure that future technologies benefit everyone, regardless of their abilities or needs. This section discusses the importance of accessibility and inclusion in graphics technology and provides insights into how developers and researchers can work towards creating more inclusive solutions.

1. Accessibility Matters

Accessibility in graphics technology involves making software, applications, and content usable by individuals with disabilities. This includes considerations for those with visual, auditory, motor, or cognitive impairments. Accessibility ensures that everyone can enjoy and benefit from technology.

2. Legal and Ethical Obligations

Many countries have laws and regulations that require digital content and applications to be accessible to people with disabilities. Ignoring these legal requirements can lead to significant consequences, including fines and legal action. Additionally, ethical considerations demand that technology is inclusive.

3. Universal Design Principles

Universal design is a guiding principle that advocates for creating products and services that are usable by the widest possible audience without the need for adaptation. Applying universal design principles to graphics technology results in interfaces and content that are more accessible to all users.

4. Testing with Diverse User Groups

To ensure inclusivity, it's essential to test graphics applications and content with diverse user groups, including individuals with disabilities. This user-centered approach helps identify barriers and challenges that may exist and allows for their resolution.

5. Accessible User Interfaces

Graphics applications should offer customizable user interfaces, including options for text size, color schemes, and keyboard shortcuts. Screen readers and other assistive technologies should be supported, and alternative text should be provided for images and multimedia content.

6. Captioning and Transcripts

Videos and audio content should include captions or transcripts to make them accessible to individuals with hearing impairments. This ensures that information is not lost to those who rely on text-based communication.

7. Keyboard Navigation

Keyboard navigation is crucial for individuals who cannot use a mouse or touchscreen. Graphics applications should provide well-defined keyboard shortcuts and a logical tab order to facilitate navigation and interaction.

8. Performance Considerations

Optimizing graphics applications for performance is essential for users with limited hardware or network connectivity. Slow-loading or resource-intensive content can exclude individuals with less capable devices.

9. User Feedback and Continuous Improvement

Encouraging user feedback and actively seeking input from individuals with disabilities is a valuable practice. This feedback can drive ongoing improvements to accessibility features and overall inclusivity.

10. Education and Awareness

Raising awareness about the importance of accessibility and inclusion in graphics technology is essential. Developers, designers, and content creators should receive training and resources to help them understand and implement accessibility best practices.

11. Inclusive Design Resources

There are many resources available for individuals and organizations interested in inclusive design. These resources include guidelines, toolkits, and accessibility testing tools that can aid in creating more inclusive graphics technology.

12. Inclusivity as a Competitive Advantage

Inclusivity can be a competitive advantage in the graphics technology industry. Products and services that prioritize accessibility can reach a broader audience and foster customer loyalty.

13. Future-Proofing Technology

Prioritizing inclusivity today ensures that graphics technology remains relevant and valuable in the future. As technology evolves, it should continue to meet the needs of all users, including those with disabilities.

In conclusion, ensuring that future graphics technology is inclusive is both a legal requirement and a moral obligation. By following accessibility best practices, conducting inclusive testing, and prioritizing user feedback, developers and researchers can create graphics technology that benefits everyone, regardless of their abilities or needs. An inclusive approach not only meets legal and ethical obligations but also enhances the quality and reach of graphics technology solutions.

Chapter 20: Final Project: Building a Graphics Tech Demo

Section 20.1: Brainstorming Cutting-edge Ideas

In this final chapter, we embark on a journey to create a cutting-edge graphics tech demo that showcases the skills and knowledge acquired throughout this book. Building a tech demo is an exciting opportunity to experiment with the latest graphics techniques and technologies, push the boundaries of what is possible, and leave a lasting impression on your audience.

1. Setting Your Objectives

Before diving into the technical details, it's crucial to define the objectives of your tech demo. What do you want to achieve with this project? Are you aiming to demonstrate a particular graphics technique, showcase your creativity, or highlight the capabilities of a specific platform or hardware? Clearly outlining your goals will guide your project's development.

2. Choosing a Theme or Concept

The theme or concept of your tech demo plays a significant role in its appeal. Whether it's a futuristic cityscape, an enchanted forest, a sci-fi spaceship, or an abstract art piece, choose a theme that resonates with your vision and target audience. Consider what visual elements, effects, and interactions will best convey your chosen theme.

3. Selecting Graphics Techniques

Leverage the knowledge gained from the preceding chapters to select the graphics techniques that will make your demo stand out. This could include real-time ray tracing, advanced shaders, particle systems, or any other cutting-edge technology that aligns with your objectives.

4. Optimizing Performance

While pushing the graphical boundaries is essential, maintaining smooth and responsive performance is equally critical. Optimization techniques discussed earlier in the book, such as GPU profiling, batching, and LOD, will help ensure your demo runs smoothly on a variety of hardware configurations.

5. Creating Engaging Interactions

Interactivity can significantly enhance the impact of your tech demo. Consider how users will interact with your scene or application. Will you implement user-driven camera controls, interactive elements, or innovative user interfaces?

6. Incorporating Audio

Don't overlook the importance of audio in your tech demo. Immersive audio techniques from Chapter 10 can complement the visuals and create a more captivating experience.

7. Implementing Real-time Elements

Real-time elements, such as dynamic weather, day-night cycles, or physics simulations, can add depth and realism to your demo. Utilize the knowledge from previous chapters to incorporate these elements seamlessly.

8. Showcasing Your Work

Consider how you'll showcase your tech demo. Will you create a standalone application, a web-based experience, or a VR/AR presentation? Your choice of platform will impact the accessibility and reach of your project.

9. Documenting Your Process

Throughout the development of your tech demo, document your progress, challenges, and solutions. This documentation can serve as a valuable resource for future projects and as a portfolio piece to showcase your skills.

10. Iterating and Polishing

The development of a tech demo is an iterative process. Continuously test, gather feedback, and refine your project to achieve the desired level of quality and impact.

11. Seeking Inspiration

Look to the works of other artists, developers, and tech enthusiasts for inspiration. Analyze what makes their projects engaging and innovative, and consider how you can incorporate similar elements into your demo.

12. Collaboration and Feedback

Don't hesitate to collaborate with others, whether they are fellow developers, artists, or audio engineers. Diverse perspectives can lead to more creative and polished results. Seek feedback from peers and mentors to refine your project further.

13. Planning for Future Exploration

Finally, remember that your tech demo is not just a culmination of your skills but a stepping stone for future explorations in the world of graphics technology. The knowledge and experience gained from this project will open doors to exciting opportunities in the field.

In Section 20.2, we will delve deeper into the technical aspects of building your graphics tech demo. So, let your creativity flow, set your objectives, and get ready to embark on this exciting journey of creating an impressive graphics tech demo.

Section 20.2: Delving into Technical Implementation

Now that we have a clear understanding of the objectives and theme for our graphics tech demo, it's time to dive into the technical implementation. This section will guide you through the key technical aspects and considerations involved in creating an impressive and cutting-edge demo.

1. Choosing the Right Graphics API

The choice of graphics API, such as OpenGL, Vulkan, or DirectX, will heavily influence your project's development. Consider the platform you intend to target and the features required for your demo. For maximum flexibility and performance, modern APIs like Vulkan or DirectX 12 are excellent choices.

2. Graphics Engine or Framework

Depending on the complexity of your demo, you might want to consider using an existing graphics engine or framework. Engines like Unity or Unreal Engine offer powerful tools for creating graphics-intensive applications. However, if you prefer more control over the rendering pipeline, building your custom engine from scratch may be the way to go.

3. Shader Programming

Shaders are the backbone of real-time graphics. Ensure you have a strong grasp of shader programming, including vertex, fragment, and compute shaders. Utilize advanced techniques covered in earlier chapters to create stunning visual effects.

4. Real-time Ray Tracing

If your demo aims to showcase cutting-edge visuals, consider integrating real-time ray tracing. Leverage the techniques discussed in Chapter 7 to implement ray tracing for reflections, shadows, and global illumination.

5. *Physics and Simulation*

Realistic physics and simulations can greatly enhance the authenticity of your demo. Implement fluid dynamics, rigid body physics, or soft body simulations using techniques from Chapter 5. Integrating NVIDIA PhysX or similar physics engines can expedite this process.

6. *Asset Creation and Optimization*

Pay careful attention to 3D asset creation and optimization. Use tools like Blender or Maya to create 3D models, and ensure they are well-optimized for real-time rendering. Techniques from Chapter 1 can help you profile and optimize your assets.

7. *Interactivity and User Interface*

Implement user interactions and intuitive user interfaces. Whether it's controlling the camera, toggling visual effects, or navigating through scenes, make sure users can engage with your demo seamlessly.

8. *Audio Integration*

Enhance the immersive experience with high-quality audio. Utilize 3D audio techniques from Chapter 10 to create spatial soundscapes that complement the visuals.

9. Multiplatform Considerations

If you plan to target multiple platforms (PC, console, VR, AR), adapt your codebase to ensure compatibility and performance optimization for each platform.

10. Optimization and Performance Profiling

Consistently optimize your codebase using profiling tools and techniques from Chapter 1. Maintain a balance between visual fidelity and performance to ensure a smooth experience on various hardware configurations.

11. Version Control and Collaboration

Implement version control using tools like Git to manage your project's source code effectively. Collaborate with team members or contributors to divide tasks and streamline development.

12. Testing and Quality Assurance

Rigorous testing is crucial. Ensure your demo is thoroughly tested on different hardware setups and platforms to identify and resolve any compatibility issues or bugs.

13. Documentation and User Guides

Create comprehensive documentation and user guides to help users navigate and understand your tech demo. This will also serve as a valuable resource for potential collaborators or contributors.

14. Legal Considerations

If your tech demo includes assets, code, or technologies created by others, ensure you have the necessary permissions, licenses, or attributions to use them legally.

15. Future-Proofing and Updates

Plan for the future by designing your codebase to be easily extensible and maintainable. Consider how you'll release updates or enhancements to keep your tech demo relevant.

16. Showcasing and Distribution

Decide how you'll showcase and distribute your tech demo. Options include hosting it on a website, submitting it to app stores, or presenting it at conferences and exhibitions.

As you delve into the technical implementation of your graphics tech demo, remember that this is a unique opportunity to push the boundaries of your skills and create something truly remarkable. Stay creative, stay focused, and enjoy the journey of bringing your vision to life.

Section 20.3: Design Considerations for Modern Hardware

In the final stages of creating your graphics tech demo, it's essential to pay special attention to design considerations that cater to modern hardware capabilities. Modern GPUs and CPUs offer impressive performance, and to fully leverage these capabilities, you must optimize your demo accordingly.

1. GPU Parallelism and Multi-threading

Modern GPUs are highly parallel processors, and taking advantage of this parallelism is crucial for achieving optimal performance. Utilize multi-threading techniques to distribute rendering tasks across multiple CPU cores, freeing up the GPU for compute-intensive tasks.

```
// Example using C++ and std::thread for multi-threading

std::thread renderThread(RenderFunction);

std::thread physicsThread(PhysicsFunction);

renderThread.join();

physicsThread.join();
```

2. Asynchronous Compute

Many modern GPUs support asynchronous compute, allowing you to overlap compute and rendering tasks. This can significantly improve overall throughput. Implement compute shaders to offload non-graphics calculations to the GPU.

```
// Example compute shader in GLSL

layout(local_size_x = 256, local_size_y = 1, local_size_z = 1) in;

buffer<float> Data;

void main() {
// Perform compute operations here

}
```

3. Dynamic Level of Detail (LOD)

Dynamic LOD systems adjust the level of detail based on the viewer's distance from objects. Implement LOD techniques from Chapter 2 to optimize the rendering of complex scenes, ensuring that resources are allocated efficiently.

4. Texture Streaming

For large textures or environments, consider implementing texture streaming. Load only the textures needed for the current scene, dynamically loading and unloading textures as the camera moves. This minimizes memory usage and improves loading times.

5. Real-time Ray Tracing Optimization

If your demo features real-time ray tracing, leverage hardware acceleration features provided by modern GPUs. Use ray tracing cores and BVH (Bounding Volume Hierarchy) acceleration structures for faster ray intersection tests.

6. GPU Memory Management

Be mindful of GPU memory usage. Implement texture compression and use techniques like texture atlases to reduce memory consumption. Monitor GPU memory usage to avoid exceeding available resources.

7. Modern Rendering APIs

If you're targeting high-performance platforms, consider using modern rendering APIs like Vulkan or DirectX 12. These APIs provide fine-grained control over the rendering pipeline and can lead to significant performance gains.

8. Real-time Ray Tracing Denoising

Real-time ray tracing can introduce noise. Implement denoising techniques from Chapter 7 to produce visually pleasing results while maintaining real-time performance.

9. High-refresh-rate Displays

If your demo supports high-refresh-rate displays (e.g., 120Hz, 144Hz), ensure that it runs smoothly at these rates. Implement adaptive sync technologies like G-Sync or FreeSync for tear-free rendering.

10. VR and AR Optimization

For VR and AR experiences, maintain consistent frame rates to prevent motion sickness. Optimize rendering for stereo views and minimize latency.

11. Cross-Platform Compatibility

If your demo targets multiple platforms, be prepared for platform-specific optimizations. Different hardware architectures may require specific rendering techniques or optimizations.

12. Benchmarking and Testing

Continuously benchmark and test your demo on a variety of hardware configurations to ensure a consistent and high-quality experience for users.

13. Resource Loading and Streaming

Optimize the loading and streaming of 3D models, textures, and assets to minimize load times and maintain smooth gameplay.

14. Content Streaming

Consider implementing content streaming techniques to reduce initial download or installation sizes, allowing users to start experiencing your demo more quickly.

As you fine-tune your graphics tech demo for modern hardware, keep in mind that optimization is an iterative process. Regularly profile and benchmark your code to identify performance bottlenecks, and don't hesitate to revisit earlier sections of this book for specific optimization techniques. Your commitment to optimization will result in a polished and impressive graphics tech demo that showcases your skills and creativity to the fullest.

Section 20.4: Presentation and Showcasing

Creating a graphics tech demo is a significant achievement, but presenting and showcasing it effectively is equally important. This section will guide you through the best practices for presenting your demo to an audience, whether it's potential employers, clients, or the gaming community.

1. Demo Reel and Trailer

Consider creating a captivating demo reel or trailer that highlights the most impressive aspects of your tech demo. Use this reel to generate interest and excitement about your work. Use video editing software to compile footage from your demo, add music, and create a polished video.

!\[Demo Reel\]\(demo_reel_thumbnail.jpg\)

Figure 1: Thumbnail for your demo reel or trailer.

2. Website or Portfolio

Build a professional website or online portfolio to showcase your tech demo. Include detailed information about your project, its features, and how it was developed. Provide download links or access instructions if applicable.

3. Live Demonstrations

Whenever possible, offer live demonstrations of your tech demo at industry events, conferences, or online streaming platforms. Interacting with your demo in real-time can leave a lasting impression on your audience.

4. Engage on Social Media

Promote your tech demo on social media platforms like Twitter, Facebook, Instagram, or specialized gaming forums. Share development updates, screenshots, and engage with your audience by responding to comments and feedback.

"Tech Demo Showcase Event! ◇

Join us on *[Date]* for a live demonstration of our graphics tech demo. We'll explore the stunning visuals and innovative features that make this project truly exceptional. Don't miss it! #TechDemoShowcase #GameDev

5. Developer Diaries

Create developer diaries or blog posts to document the journey of creating your tech demo. Share insights, challenges, and breakthroughs. This not only helps others learn from your experience but also humanizes your project.

6. Press Releases and Reviews

Write a press release to announce the release of your tech demo. Reach out to gaming news websites and influencers for reviews and coverage. Positive reviews can significantly boost your project's visibility.

7. Feedback and Iteration

Encourage users to provide feedback on your tech demo. Use this feedback to make improvements and release updates. Regular updates can keep your project relevant and attract more users over time.

8. Community Engagement

If your tech demo gains a following, consider creating a dedicated community forum or Discord server. Engage with your community, address their questions, and foster a sense of belonging among your users.

9. Contests and Awards

Submit your tech demo to game development contests and awards. Winning or even being nominated for such awards can significantly enhance your project's reputation.

10. Documentation

Provide comprehensive documentation for your tech demo, including installation instructions, system requirements, and usage guidelines. Clear documentation makes it more accessible to a wider audience.

11. User Support

Offer reliable user support through email or community forums. Promptly address technical issues or questions that users may encounter.

12. Networking

Attend game development conferences, meetups, and networking events. Building connections in the industry can lead to collaboration opportunities or job offers.

13. Monetization Strategy

If your tech demo is commercial, have a clear monetization strategy in place. Decide on pricing, distribution platforms, and marketing campaigns to maximize sales.

14. Intellectual Property

Ensure that you have appropriate licenses for any third-party assets used in your tech demo. Protect your own intellectual property rights as well.

15. Transparency

Be transparent about the limitations and scope of your tech demo. This helps manage user expectations and prevents disappointment.

16. Feedback Loop

Continuously gather feedback and data on how users interact with your tech demo. Use analytics tools to track user behavior and preferences, which can inform future updates and projects.

Creating a remarkable tech demo is just the first step. Effectively presenting and promoting your work is essential for its success. By following these strategies, you can maximize the impact of your graphics tech demo and gain recognition in the industry.

Section 20.5: Reflections and Future Exploration

As you near the end of your journey in creating a graphics tech demo, it's essential to reflect on what you've learned and consider the possibilities for future exploration in the field of graphics programming.

1. Lessons Learned

Reflect on the challenges you faced and the solutions you devised during the development of your tech demo. Documenting these lessons learned will be invaluable for your growth as a graphics programmer.

2. Feedback Analysis

Analyze the feedback and responses you received from users, peers, and the community. What aspects of your tech demo received praise, and where were the pain points? Use this feedback to make informed decisions in future projects.

3. New Technologies

Stay up-to-date with the latest graphics programming technologies and trends. Explore emerging technologies such as ray tracing, machine learning, and real-time rendering advancements. Consider how these technologies can enhance your future projects.

4. Further Optimization

Graphics programming often involves optimizing for performance. Explore advanced optimization techniques, such as parallel computing, multithreading, and hardware-specific optimizations, to make your graphics applications even more efficient.

5. Cross-Platform Development

If your tech demo was primarily developed for a specific platform, consider expanding to other platforms such as consoles, mobile devices, or web-based solutions. Understanding cross-platform development can broaden your career opportunities.

6. Advanced Rendering Techniques

Dive deeper into advanced rendering techniques like physically-based rendering (PBR), global illumination, and procedural generation of textures and environments. Mastering these techniques can lead to breathtaking visual experiences.

7. Artificial Intelligence

Explore the intersection of graphics and artificial intelligence (AI). Incorporate AI-driven characters, behaviors, and procedural content generation into your projects for more dynamic and immersive experiences.

8. Real-time Ray Tracing

As real-time ray tracing becomes more accessible, delve into its implementation and its potential to revolutionize rendering quality in games and simulations.

9. Simulation Realism

If your interests lean towards simulation, explore more realistic simulations of physics, weather, and complex systems. These can be applied in gaming, scientific visualization, and engineering fields.

10. Interdisciplinary Collaboration

Collaborate with professionals from diverse fields, such as artists, musicians, and scientists, to create interdisciplinary projects that push the boundaries of graphics technology.

11. Teaching and Sharing Knowledge

Consider sharing your knowledge and expertise by teaching graphics programming, writing tutorials, or contributing to open-source projects. Teaching can deepen your understanding of the subject and give back to the community.

12. Ethics and Inclusion

Explore the ethical implications of graphics technology and consider how you can contribute to making technology more inclusive and accessible to all. Champion diversity and inclusion in your projects and the industry.

13. Mentorship

If you have gained substantial experience, consider mentoring aspiring graphics programmers. Mentorship can be a fulfilling way to give back to the community and help others succeed.

14. Continuous Learning

Graphics programming is a field that continually evolves. Commit to lifelong learning and staying curious about new developments in computer graphics.

15. *Personal Growth*

Reflect on your personal and professional growth throughout this project. Recognize your achievements, and use them as motivation for future endeavors.

Your graphics tech demo is not just an endpoint but a stepping stone to a future filled with exciting possibilities. Embrace the journey of exploration and innovation in the ever-evolving world of graphics programming. Remember that every challenge you overcome and every new skill you acquire brings you closer to becoming a true expert in the field.